P 412

CW00497317

LIAISON OFFICER

To all who fought
To all who died
To all who loved

I

It was autumn 1943. The American papers were saying the war would be over soon. Having given up my teaching post in the Middle West, I'd waited a year for my passage home as an Overseas Volunteer. Although the papers kept saying we were winning, they hadn't made mention of the German subs in the Atlantic or that our convoy ships had gone down like sitting ducks; nor of the shortage of shipping to replace them. So it was a shock when I got to Boston to see the cargo boat that was to take me home to England.

The SS Olaf lay moored in the harbour: old, clumsy, dingy-grey. She looked capable of no more than ten knots even at full speed. At her masthead there was the blue cross of Norway on a faded red flag. Around her hold bren-gun carriers, each covered in canvas, stood lashed awkwardly to the deck. Grain spilt from the loading of her cargo of foodstuffs littered the boards.

I met the other passengers at dinner that night—the elderly American Howells; Lady Chilbeame returning from three years' residence in the States; Ellen, a red-haired American girl married to an English sailor and now setting out to join him in Plymouth. And George. The meal over and the Norwegian captain and officers having left us, we sat in the lounge dallying with our coffee and brandy.

"It's a disgrace," fumed Howells, "for them to send us on a Norwegian ship. I shall report this when I get to the other side. By God, I shall."

"*If* we get to the other side," murmured Ellen. George crossed himself.

Howells fumbled in his breast pocket and produced a bundle of crowned and crested documents.

"You see these letters? They're all from cabinet ministers, the Minister for Food, the Minister of State for War. That's what they think of me in England. I'm engaged to do a big job for them reorganising your NAAFI service—do you know I own a chain of hotels in Chicago and throughout the Middle West? Well, *that's* the expertise I'm putting at the disposal of your government. It's a big job, boy, and I don't expect to be treated like—like some anonymous private who's simply going over there as cannon fodder for an army that's damn well not fighting."

"Thanks," I said. I was due to be one of those anonymous privates once we got over to Europe, and I wasn't so crazy about all that fighting as he was. Nor, I could see, was George.

George was half British, half Mexican. Short, swarthy, he had brown mournful eyes and a round face. His hair was cropped in an American crewcut, very black, with already a fleck of Mexican silver in it. He was about my age, in his mid to late twenties. Although he shaved close around his heavy jowl, stubble sprang up in obstinate leaden patches. Beneath his forehead, creasing into long anxious folds, his face was sad and gentle.

Everything about the ship amazed him. He had never seen an ocean-going vessel before, his life having been passed in a small and remote mountain village, where his father, a Scot, had worked as chief mining engineer. Thirty years, George told us, with never a visit on leave back to the old country. He had a large family—ten children, of whom George was the eldest—and he left their upbringing to his Mexican wife, while he concerned himself with his work at the mine. But he had a second love, which grew as the years passed.

8

"My father also loved Britain," George told us with pride.

Sipping our brandy—the Norwegians had plenty of liquor on board—we let George go on talking, while we nodded sympathetically and tried to imagine a gaunt old Scots engineer who had gone native while his heart yearned all the time for the mother country that he was never to see again. Around him ten clamouring Mexican children, the seed of his loins, but the image of their mother.

"It was always my father's wish to return to the Old Country one day. He would take us all to see Buckingham Palace, and the King and Queen as they rode in the streets. And the Lord Mayor of London, because London, as you know, is the capital of the world—

"Huh!" exclaimed Ellen.

Lady Chilbeame flashed her an indignant look.

Chewing on the wet end of his Havana, Howells said, "It used to be. Used to be."

"To him it was the capital of the world," George said almost pleadingly, unnerved by the unexpected argument.

Turning to him, Lady Chilbeame put on her most gracious look. "He must have been a very sweet man."

George glowed with pride. "He loved Britain with all his heart. He would let no one at home say a bad thing about his country. No one wanted to, and no one dared to. He was British, and I too am British."

"Half British," put in Howells.

"No, I am British. I go to fight for Britain."

"Well, so do I, so do we all—in our different ways—but that doesn't make us British. I mean Ellen's not British, never will be, she's a true Yankee, aren't you, dear?"

"Sure am. Marrying a Limey won't make me a Limey, you bet it won't."

"The Stars and Stripes for ever," grinned Howells.

Howells lifted his brandy. Ellen and he clinked glasses together, tinkling out of existence Lady Chilbeame's discreetly supercilious smile.

"The Bible and the Union Jack," George went on, "these things he taught us to respect. The Bible he kept on his desk in the—the drawing room, I think you call it. The Union Jack flew always from a flagpole on the roof. Every night one of us boys lowered it and every morning our father hoisted it first thing. It flew there every day for thirty years." George stopped to smile at us. His teeth shone white against his swarthy face and black stubbly chin.

"Splendid," said Lady Chilbeame. "Absolutely splendid, the very best type of pioneer."

"And that is how I, George Andres Pedro Jesus Mc-Naughton, come to be with you sailing to England to help the Old Country."

He looked around for our approbation; but Lady Chilbeame's applause had improvidently already spent itself. Howells and Ellen merely looked at each other and shrugged.

"Do you mean to say," put in Howells, "that you are volunteering for a foreign army just because your old man ran a Union Jack up on a flagpole every day in some Godforsaken Mexican mining village inhabited by a lot of ignorant peasants?"

"You are a Yanqui, so you do not understand."

"Not just for a flag on a flagpole?" Howells pressed.

George reddened beneath his dark skin. "You come to England because of a big contract. You have the Minister of Food pay you many thousands of dollars. But I come because I make a solemn promise."

"Promise," sniffed Howells like a dog on the scent. "What sort of promise?"

"I swore a sacred oath that I will help my father's country in her hour of need. I keep promise. I want nothing from the country I go to serve." He was very excited. "This is more than a flag upon a flagpole. This is a solemn promise I give to my father when he lay dying."

"Poppycock," puffed Howells.

"Pipe down," said Ellen, turning on him. "Go on, George, you tell us about it and don't pay any attention to Big-Mouth here."

"It was a promise to my father." As he spoke, you could tell that the incident cast a romantic glow over his own actions that gave him a sense of importance and self-confidence.

"I am the eldest of his children. When he was dying he sent for me. He lay in his bed and my mother was weeping, so he sent her out of the room. The priest was there at the bedside. My father was not of his religion, but that did not matter, it was my mother's religion and mine, and the candles were burning in the room. He was very ill, you understand, and we all knew that he was dying. He had asked me in to give me his blessing. But first 'Will you make me a promise?' he said.

"'I do what you want me to do,' I said.

"'I want you to promise that you will not let your mother make you forget that you are British.'

"'I shall not forget it,' I said.

"'You are my eldest. When I die you will be left alone to take charge of the family. You are to take my place, do you understand?'

"'I understand,' I said.

"'You will take my place, not your mother. You will be head of the family. She is a fine woman, and you are to love and respect her, but she is a Mexican woman. Whereas you are my son, George; you must do what I would do.'

"'I will try,' I told him, 'always to do what you would do.'

"'I have one last promise for you to make,' he said. 'I want you to swear in front of Father Basilio here that if your country—that is Britain, George, not Mexico—if your country is in danger you will go to her help, just as I would do. I mean if there is war'."

As we sat in the ship's gloomy lounge, I imagined that deathbed scene, with the candles burning and the priest hovering near to catch the words that passed between father and son.

"I am my father's eldest son, so I promise." Once again George looked round at us proudly. "I think he was a prophet, because a few months after he died England is at war. So I come to fight for England and I keep my promise."

"It's sure taken you a few years to do it," drawled Howells sourly. He was clearly put out. His salary and his chain of hotels and his contacts high up in London somehow now seemed the mercenary things we had known all along they were. Sensing our hostility, he got up irritably and stalked out onto the deck.

"He's jealous. Say, George, you're quite a guy, I reckon." Ellen clinked her glass with his.

"To George," said Lady Chilbeame, lifting her glass to mine.

When we sailed from Boston, after nearly a week in harbour, we headed for Halifax, Nova Scotia, hugging the coastline, and covered by constant air patrols. The voyage was slow, cramped and uncomfortable, but the excitement of travelling did something to erase the ill-temper and bickering which had grown on us at Boston. Unfortunately, the journey to Halifax was soon accomplished, and there in that vast and spacious inner pool, with its beautiful landscape at our rear, we tied up for nobody knew how long.

"Convoy," said the Norwegian captain gloomily, "has to assemble."

Our boredom and irritation returned and we had nothing to do but wait on board. During the day we sat on deck in blazing sunshine and looked across the water to the other cargo ships gathered there at anchor, bearing the flags of every allied nationality, as well as some (like the Swedish ships) that were neutral. Lined up all round us were flotillas of corvettes.

Beyond the harbour itself was the town and beyond the town the hilly slopes of Nova Scotia.

Only Howells kept busy. He was a dapper little man, who could talk to all sorts of people easily. Because he was interested in things and the working of things, he knew how to ask questions about them. It was this capacity which won people's confidence in him at first. When a crew of British ack-ack gunners came aboard to man the two Bofors guns which were the ship's only protection against air attack, he soon ingratiated himself with them. He sympathised with them in their grievances—Norwegian food, for instance, and language difficulties—and egged them on against the Norwegians. Then I overheard him talking to the Norwegian crew, setting them off against the 'snooty Limey gunners'. When the friction thus aroused showed signs of temporarily abating, other causes seemed to spring to life for his restless ego to work upon. He set the Norwegian crew against their officers. And then the Norwegian captain against the British convoy admiral, blaming him for our long delay in harbour.

As we sat there on deck on an autumn afternoon, we were all affected by frustration in various ways. Howells was fuming at one more delay before he could set about his work in England and make his presence felt at the very highest levels. Lady Chilbeame was dreaming of the church spires and little hedgerows of the Pytchley countryside. Ellen was beguiling the boredom of waiting by a flirtation with the second officer. George was warding off homesickness for the hot, dry, rarefied air of Mexico, buoyed by the vision of himself as a new St. George riding on a Norwegian charger to England's aid. His was a lovely long dream of paternal approbation blessed by all the saints of his church and falling into place amid vague notions of hidalgo honour.

The Norwegian steward brought us a pot of tea and some buttered toast with strawberry jam. He had a scar low on his cheek which made him seem to grin always. Yet clearly he was happy to be in port; there were too many subs in the Atlantic for him to be otherwise. Grinning thus, he busied himself with treating us like cabin passengers on some peaceful round the world cruise.

Just as though we were on a picnic ashore, two or three wasps began to buzz round our plates. Their little tigerish bodies disturbed our peace; they became small enemy irritants that failed to respect our privacy and ignored our human power. Howells swatted one with his hat; it was a stunning but not a deadly blow. The creature dropped to the boards of the deck by George's foot. George gazed at it, watching its feeble struggling not more than two inches from the toe of his right shoe.

"Kill it," ordered Howells.

"Oh, do get rid of the beastly thing," cried Lady C.

George smiled wanly. He fumbled in his pocket and produced an old envelope. Bending down towards the deck he endeavoured to shovel the wasp onto the envelope. His intention clearly was to lift it to the deck rail and tip it overboard.

"Tread on it!" Howells leaped up and in a couple of strides reached George's chair. His foot came down with a stamp, and when he removed it the wasp was squelched in a semi-liquid mess on the clean deck boards.

"Look, here's another," said Howells. "Kill it, George, come on, George, you kill this one."

The wasp was some feet away, and Howells grabbed George by the arm.

"Kill it, George."

"Please," appealed Lady Chilbeame, "I can't stand wasps."

"Kill it, you little coward."

George jumped up. "I no kill," he shouted, and bent down with his little blue envelope once more. Collecting the jammy-legged wasp sticking precariously to its edge, he rushed to the deck rail and threw wasp and envelope alike over the side. The envelope fluttered down into the greeny-blue water, the wasp flew away. George sat down with a thump. He seemed to shrink into the canvas of the chair. "I no kill," he muttered back at us.

"You no kill, you dirty little grease-ball," cried Howells. "You no kill wasps, you no kill Germans either. What good do you think *you'll* be to His Majesty's forces? What are you going to do when a Nazi soldier comes to you and you've got a bayonet in your hands—are you going to drive it into his guts or not? When you hear it squelch as it goes in, are you going to give it a twist round in his belly? Or are you going to let it stay sucked in his inside? And when his guts begin to ooze out it will make more mess than *this*."

He paused to rub his foot in the mashed smear that was all that was left of the original wasp. "Or are you going to cry 'I no kill' and let him drive his bayonet into *you* and smear *your* guts around with his swizzle stick?"

"Please," protested Lady Chilbeame.

"Well, tell us, you half-caste wet bag, don't just sit there shrivelled up in your chair, tell us."

"I no kill." Over the rail one could see the water down below swirling in ugly currents against the ship's side. "I fight, but I no kill."

"How the hell can you fight, man, and not kill?"

"I fight in the RAF. I no fight with bayonet. I fly a plane in the sky." He pointed, becoming more animated, to the immaculate Madonna-blue sky above us.

"Sure," said Ellen bitterly, "it's clean up there, no mess up there."

"Oh, yes, there is," said Howells. "Fire, burning. Plunging down, George, thousands of feet, and burning to death all the way. You can be roasted so bad up there you'll wish you had a simple end like a Hun putting a bayonet straight into your belly. You'll be crying out up there for a quick and simple death."

"Please," said Lady Chilbeame. "You've distressed him

enough, there's no need to distress us all."

"Lady, this guy is just jelly with fear. Look at him—been posing as a goddam hero coming to old England's rescue, and making all that song and dance about a promise to his dying father. When did his father die?—I'll tell you when—*before the war,* four years ago. Four damn years he's been making up his mind to keep a promise he hadn't got the guts to refuse his dying dad."

"It was a sacred promise," said George.

We hadn't expected him to say anything; it was a surprise for us that he spoke from his chair at all.

"Sacred promise be blowed. You'll turn and run, I know your kind; you'll let down the men who are with you—up in the air or on the ground, it makes no difference. You shouldn't be allowed to do it." He was struck by a sudden thought. "And by God I'll see you won't. I'm going to report on this voyage to the Secretary of State for War and when I do, I'll ask him to see that you never even get accepted for the forces."

He turned and left us, satisfied with his destruction.

"I think," said Lady Chilbeame, "I shall go to my cabin."

Ellen stood up and stretched her strawberry freckled arms. "See you later," she said, "I've got a date with the second mate."

George got up, his body sagged and his legs carried him weakly to the stern of the ship. He leaned against the gunwale, bending his head in his hands. I had a feeling he might be contemplating throwing himself over, but he remained still.

The next day we sailed in a sixty ship convoy, an armada laden with grain and bren-gun carriers, steaming slowly into the Atlantic, smoke puffing and chuffing from our funnels and each ship like a fat, middle-aged lady waddling to catch a bus, an awkwardness of metal in a flat calm of sea. National flags were flying from the ships' masts—British, American, Free French, Netherlands, Danish, Icelandic, Greek, Norwegian, Swedish. Destroyers escorted us, corvettes slipped round our flanks, an aircraft carrier hovered watchfully near and from Newfoundland planes patrolled ahead. We sailed at ten knots.

"Northern route," the captain told us with a kind of taciturn relish at dinner that night. To arc up in the cold, grey, dead northern wastes of sea seemed to please his Viking spirit. "Towards Iceland." He swept vaguely with his hand. "A long way, but very safe."

"How long?" inquired Howells.

The captain calculated slowly, placing his spoon back carefully into his soup. He was a very old man and everything he did now was slow. "Two weeks," he decided.

"Oh my God," said Howells to us, "can you imagine it? Two whole weeks on board this tub travelling at ten knots. A fortnight wasted already between Boston and Halifax, and now we go the longest route in the slowest convoy."

"Ah," said the captain, not properly understanding all he said, "I agree with you. Convoys is bad. Bad and slow. Leave it to me, and I would take the ship straight across. I risk the U-boats. Last convoy sixty-nine ships set off, twenty-two arrive. U-boats destroy one ship only when it sails alone, but the whole convoy when they go together."

"Oh, but the convoys have the protection of the Royal Navy," interposed Lady Chilbeame. "Without that no boats could safely cross at all."

The captain's grizzled beard and long yellow moustache twitched contemptuously.

"I tell you we are better off without protection. Let the neutral Swedish ships have protection. They have a yellow cross in their flag and a yellow streak also in their character. Let Swedish ships have protection; they won't fight, they need a convoy. *We* are not cowards." He paused and glared around. I saw George flinch under his gaze. And somehow everyone else seemed to look at George at the same instant.

"We are Norwegians and we have the sea in our blood, so we are not afraid of the German U-boats and we are not afraid to die in the water."

"But what about your cargo?" objected Ellen. "What about the people in Britain waiting for supplies from the US?"

"I tell you," said the old man, roused, "one voyage when convoys was just beginning, there were twenty ships, all nationalities—but no Swedes. That *was* a convoy. A British Admiral come to take command when we get near Europe. We have to sail to England past Ireland. It becomes very foggy. The admiral sends a message that we go into this great bay." The old man began chuckling and splashing his soup in its bowl on to his faded blue jacket. "It is very foggy so I get lost. My ship, you understand, it does not go into the bay, I steam straight ahead to England. This way I save perhaps one day's journey. I get the cargo to Liverpool safe and on time. That is good seamanship, to get the ship and the cargo home safe and in the shortest time." The rheum began to water in his eyes as he laughed.

"But what happened," asked Lady Chilbeame, "I mean, what did the admiral say?"

The captain burst into roars of laughter; he looked at the mate and the mate burst into an answering roar.

Then suddenly the captain sobered up. "He sink," he said angrily. "He drown, and all that convoy, they all sink. U-boats get them all in the bay. Only I get through, because I disobey. I say I get lost in the fog, but I disobey. I am a seaman, always a good seaman will beat the U-boats. And we Norwegians are better seamen than the Germans. That is why we shall win this war."

"I trust," said Lady Chilbeame anxiously, "that you have no intention of leaving *this* convoy."

The old man chuckled. "No, no," he reassured her. "Now we have to accept. We do not like, but we accept. Once perhaps with much fog and not so many U-boats it was possible, but now I must travel with a crazy Greek ship on one side and a Swede on the other. What an end to a sailor's life! This is what makes war a disgrace today."

"There's some pretty thick fog outside right now," Howells said.

"Always off Newfoundland there is fog." He went on with his dinner, mumbling and gnawing through his food, saying little more, absorbed in his thoughts.

Up on deck thick mists swirled like silent, shapeless waves of the sea, weaving dark and shifting patterns around the superstructure of the deck. I clutched at a half-seen iron handrail; it was cold and wet. A few yards from me there was a tiny red glow which moved and flickered. I shuffled my way along the handrail towards it and found that it turned into the dark shape of a man smoking. It was George.

I took the lighted cigarette from him and threw it into the sea. "Black-out," I reminded him. "One little light is all a U-boat needs. In this fog he could come up inside the convoy and pick us off ship by ship."

"I don't feel so good," George muttered.

I could feel the pounding throb of the engines strumming on my stomach nerves, and I suddenly remembered that George had never been to sea before in his life.

"Come on, George. Remember your father—how proud he'd be."

"No, sir. It give me no pleasure any more. Your Mr. Howells was right. He show me that I am coward."

"Listen, George, this is the sea sickness making you feel like this. Everybody feels a coward when they are sea sick."

"I don' know this sea sickness what you talk about. I know that everybody hates me, because your Mr. Howells shows everybody that I live a lie. I don' want to go to England."

"But you volunteered, George. That's no lie, that actually happened. You did it, no one made you—"

"Father Basilio made me. He said I must keep my

19

promise."

"It shows much courage that you keep such a promise."

"I don' want to keep my promise. I don' want to fight and I don' want to die."

"We're all frightened, each one of us. I'm frightened—"

"Mr. Howells, he's not frightened."

"He's terrified. He's frightened that people in England won't think he's important, that they won't know what a big shot he is."

I could feel George hesitate as he thought over my answer.

"You don' think I am a coward?"

But, in that very fraction of a second that I paused, my answer was anticipated by a sound which boomed through the fog. Deep, harsh, explosive; it sounded close. As the fog curled round us from all sides, we could see nothing, but this muffled boom seemed to come from the ship's stern.

"What's that?" said George, with alarm.

"Depth charges." I took his arm and began to move quickly towards the companion way. He looked at me uncomprehendingly as we descended into the light. "That means subs are around. Get your life-jacket on."

In the lounge Howells was already wrapping his jacket around his chest. "I bet that little swine's been smoking on deck again," he burst out. "Do you know that a match can be seen at three miles' distance?"

"In fog?" I said.

"Oh—, do help me with this thing," cried Lady Chilbeame.

"The American girl," shouted Howells, "where the hell is she?"

Lady C. coughed discreetly. "I think she is in her cabin." But Howells was already banging at the door.

I looked at my life-jacket; the canvas was a dirty, faded grey, it looked as though it was at least a generation old, and the cork was worn and crumbly, rotten.

"What do you want?" Ellen was shouting back through the

locked door.

"You can come out or stay," called Howells. "Whether you drown or not is your affair. But I want discipline on board this ship, and that means behaving properly in an emergency."

He was swelling with importance as he prepared to take charge, and I imagined the rest of us rowing in a lifeboat while he sat in the stern and acted as our leader.

"Go to hell," said Ellen.

"I know you've got the second mate in there," shouted Howells. "Don't you realise, man, you're needed?"

The door opened, the burly figure of the second mate stood blinking in the doorway.

"What do you want?"

"Where's your sense of duty?"

"I am not on duty. It is the captain's watch. My watch is not until the middle watch."

"Can't you hear that they're dropping depth charges, man? And do you think you ought to be in a passenger's cabin at a moment like this?"

The second mate laughed. "Oh, those. Every voyage we drop those. All day maybe—boom—boom—boom." He moved away laughing. "All day, all the time, boom—boom—boom." Ellen came out from his shadow in the doorway. "You're crazy," she told Howells, "just plain crazy." She shut her door in our faces, and we could hear her pouring herself a drink.

"Well," said Lady C. "I think that such conduct is shocking. It would never happen on a British ship. And think of that gal's husband, too. Poor boy." We sat down rather helplessly at the large table in the lounge. Howells drummed on its hard surface nervously. George looked greener than ever; the lines on his forehead seemed like ruts. He sat hunched up, as though he wanted to screw himself up into an embryonic ball.

"What a shipload," said Howells bitterly, "to be torpedoed with."

The depth charges went on all the time we were off the Newfoundland Banks. The fog lasted for at least two days. Then we began to break through it into patches of grey sky and grey sea. We could see our sister ships looming up with dangerous suddenness in the patchy mist. Sometimes the Swede seemed to veer down hugely upon us on our port side and there would be shouting and insults in Norwegian from the bridge and we would swing sharply off course to avoid a collision and that would bring us bearing down on the starboard onto the Greek ship. We could hear the Greeks shouting abuse as we checked course yet again. But by this time the Swede would be back in line, and somehow the convoy would be righted once more.

"Where there are Swedes there is always trouble," our captain growled.

George looked at us mournfully. "Why does everyone hate everybody else?"

"You start hating the Germans," advised Howells. "It helps, if you have to burst a man's guts with your bayonet. There are times when it helps to hate."

"Please," said Lady Chilbeame, "don't let's start all that again."

George looked ill. He got up and staggered out to be seasick.

For days he went on being seasick, not quite throwing up, but always on the verge. His stomach was empty but convulsive heaves shook him and sometimes a thick green bile would be vomited over the ship's rail. We got him on to the deck with difficulty, wrapped him up, and made him lie in a sheltered spot near the old paint-flaked, davit-rusted lifeboat. He just sat there or stretched out and fell asleep. When he wasn't sleeping, he gazed at us with mournful eyes. Howells, brisk and energetic, had found a route around the deck which he circled so many dozen times before and after every meal.

His route passed within touching distance of George's sheltered nest on deck, but he neither looked at him nor spoke to him as he passed. George always followed him with his eyes, but what their soulful expression meant—whether amazed, appealing, or secretly loathing—no one knew.

Howells would not speak to George. Lady Chilbeame would not speak to Ellen. Ellen wouldn't speak to either Howells or Lady Chilbeame. George was too ill or too unhappy to speak to anyone. We were seven days out from Halifax and had another seven days to go. The sky was leaden; the waters looked cold and powerful as great waves hit the boat's hull, pushing her this way and that, slap-slap. With each of these giant slaps the whole boat shuddered.

We had shaken off the long distance subs completely. But as we came nearer to Europe we could expect to meet a new pack of shorter-ranged U-boats. Howells, who mixed easily with both the Norwegian crew and the British gunners, brought us back cheerful stories of the destruction of earlier convoys.

The British gunners laughed when we wore life-jackets. And indeed after that first scare with depth charges, we were too embarrassed to display ourselves in them again. "If we're hit, I don't give a dime for our chances of remaining alive in the water for more than half an hour," said Howells, looking over the side at the restless surface and heavy depths below. "You'd freeze to death in less than that time."

"And you needn't think," he added, "that anyone's going to spend time trying to pick you up. They steam straight on. The convoy orders are: no rescue. Ships that are hit are left to their fate. The convoy steams on."

"Oh, but the destroyers," put in Lady Chilbeame.

"Too busy hunting subs to search for survivors. Too busy saving what's still afloat to worry about what's going down."

"How dreadful," she shuddered. George spewed quietly over the deck rail, and his green bile became an infinitesimal part of a vast ocean that itself resembled green bile.

Overhead, the patrolling planes from the aircraft carrier buzzed on their regular hovering search. The aircraft carrier itself floated awkwardly in the distance, a tiny yet cumbersome platform on the surface of the endless waters.

"Isn't she a beauty?" said Howells. "Do you know that the convoy before this one had no carrier? Two boats out of every three were sunk. Tankers aflame, shot down like sitting ducks, burning like acetylene lamps in the night. And the rest of the convoy steaming past, while—" he turned and grinned at Lady Chilbeame "—while officers and crew stood on the deck singing 'Land of Hope and Glory'."

"How splendid," she cried, "how absolutely splendid." Then, realising too late his irony, she turned on her heel and stalked away.

Howells now struck up an acquaintanceship with the engine room crew. For a short while the chubby, round-faced chief engineer became his confidant. After dinner one evening, I sat alone in the corner of the lounge, reading a two-year-old copy of *Reader's Digest* supplied by one of the various comforts-for-sailors organisations. I could vaguely hear Howells' voice. He was shooting his usual line about making a full report on the entire circumstances of the voyage when he reached the other side. I could just hear enough to know that this time it was the captain he was criticising.

"How old do you reckon that guy is? Seventy-three? I tell you he's still living in the days of sailing ships."

"No, no," said the chubby engineer. "He is a good seaman, a good sailor."

"Good God, man, he's up there in his cabin boozing every night, with the first mate. They sit there drinking night after night, until they're helpless. And the ship's run by a second officer who's spending all *his* time with a slut from the slums of Charleston. And by a third mate who's only just got his ticket and is hardly more than a boy."

"No, no," protested the Norwegian amiably—he was one of those slow stocky men whom it is impossible to arouse—"the skipper has the first watch. Then he is not drunk. When the first watch ends, then he drinks."

"What would happen if the ship were hit by a torpedo and the captain dead drunk?"

The engineer laughed. "If the ship is hit by a torpedo, we all drown. If we are hit, we go down. So we might as well drink, yes?" He poured himself out another glass of whiskey. "Skol," he grinned.

"He has a responsibility—"

"Ah, say no more. The captain is a good captain. He has served many years. He has always been a good captain. He is a very old man, very lonely. He drinks now because his wife is dead, and he is unhappy, and he wants to join her. But first he has to sail the ship, one journey, then another, in convoy like this, one year and then another year until the war is ended. And each voyage there is some Norwegian ship sinks, some other skipper drowns. So each year the Norwegian ships become fewer and fewer because there is no new ships that come from Norway since the Germans occupy it. And everybody tells him what to do, where he must sail, how fast he must go; and he has to keep the Swedish ship on his port side and the Greek ship always on his starboard. And on his boat, the Norwegian boat, they put a British crew of gunners, and passengers—" The engineer spread his hands expressively.

"He's not up to it and you know it," said Howells.

"No, no," said the engineer gently like an amiable child explaining things to his teacher, "this is war, so the captain drinks, and the second mate has some fun with the passenger. You see, in your country you have had no war, so you don't know that in war we live—how shall I say?—somehow different. So now we drink," he said, lifting his glass in his thick, stumpy-fingered hand, "to the end of the war. Skol."

One day we heard that the British gunners had been in a fight with the Norwegian crew. One of them had a shiny round black eye. Everybody felt quarrelsome and miserable. If only George had not been on board we might have behaved better, but when we compared ourselves to him we felt morally superior.

"That poor gunner ..." said Lady Chilbeame. "I am disappointed in the Norwegians."

"What about the Americans?" I said.

"That American girl certainly. Thank heavens she has at least had the discretion to keep her affairs to the officers. I mean, just imagine if she had set her cap at those boys in the gun crew ... her poor husband ... word does get around in the Navy, you know."

Every day passed like every other now. George, risen from his couch, leaned over the rail and gloomily watched the endless water swirl by. By night he lay in his bunk, moaning in restless nightmares. Howells had nobody left in the crew to talk to; so he began again on us.

"If only that damn Mexican would take his mournful face out of our sight, we shouldn't feel like this. I've seen some frightened people in my time, but I've never seen anyone so frightened as that guy. He's making us all think of drowning. And when he's in the RAF he'll make everyone think of death by being shot down. *If* he ever gets into the air."

"Don't tell me. You're going to have a report sent to the Air Ministry"

"You're damn right I am."

Lady Chilbeame concentrated her fury on knitting woollen comforters for the troops. Ellen was by now sharing her company with all three of the mates. The gunners huddled together in their guncrew. The Norwegian seamen no longer talked to us passengers, but passed us by without a nod. Yet to George they showed a sort of respect, such as primitive people pay to signs or symbols of ill-omen. They walked past wherever he happened to be, on a kind of shushed tip-toe, as though he were already a corpse. But they would not speak to him.

The chief engineer kept to the engine room. The captain appeared at meals only on rare occasions. His beard and moustache seemed to get yellower and yellower, his eyes more bloodshot. On the morning of the fourteenth day, however, he staggered down to breakfast. He sat grinning silently to himself as he banged the table for the steward. The steward jumped to serve him as briskly as he had on day one. It was as if they knew something we didn't.

The captain began staining his yellow moustache a dirty rust as he supped from a huge beaker full of milky cocoa. The motion of the ship seemed more regular, the thudding of the engines less strained. The lounge table was distinctly steadier than usual.

"What's happening?" Howells asked suspiciously.

"Go up on deck and you will see."

We rushed up above. There were leaden skies overhead and grim dark-grey waters below; but bounding them on the eastward, containing them like the wall of a dam, was a steep horizon of cliff. Greyer than the water, immovable against the surge of the Atlantic, a smooth, almost vertical face of rock. Above it the land reared back, massive and desolate. Straining through the binoculars, we could see little dabs of cottage gleaming white against the dark brown hillsides.

"England!" cried Lady Chilbeame, turning to me, her eyes bright and blissful. For a moment, despite our mutual antagonism and different social background, the same relief and emotion gripped us both.

"Scotland," I corrected gently.

"My God," exclaimed Ellen, appalled at the barrenness, "is it all like that?"

"No, darling," beamed Lady C., "this is Scotland. But it's *almost* like home."

Howells turned to Ellen. "Don't let them kid you, my dear, the whole bloody island's bleak from end to end. Even the inhabited parts need modernising. You'll see when you get down to Plymouth." He took her arm with ready affection, saying, "We Yanks have got to stand together against the Limeys now."

She gave his arm a squeeze and together they descended to their awaiting breakfast.

"Well," confided Lady C. "I *do* find Americans most extraordinary." As we turned to go back down too, I saw George hanging on to the rail, gazing at those stone cliffs, the stern and inhospitable frontier of his father's native land.

"Come on, George, breakfast."

He shook his head.

"You've made it, George. We're here, we're home, it's the end of the voyage."

He stood at the rail, gripping it tightly, as though the land ahead was worse than the sea which lay behind.

"The end of the voyage, George."

He was still gazing at the rock face of the land, to which we were drawing ever closer. He stood there, his despair hard and unrelenting.

"Yes," he said, "for me it is the end."

We disembarked at Leith, and were sent by officials, after interview, on our separate ways. I did not see any of them again.

II

"Well, what regiment do you want to join?" said the puffed up, blotchy-faced casualty in uniform who manned the recruiting officer's desk.

The three pips on his shoulder told me that he was a captain. His voice was irritable. Abroad, reading the patriotic stuff in the newspapers sent to me, I had learnt that the Army was so efficiently organised that a whole battery of the latest psychological tests matched the recruit to the job he was fitted for. The little captain with his ill-looking complexion did not seem exactly the embodiment of this idea.

"What would you suggest, sir?" I enquired, deferring to the experience which I felt no doubt resided within this war-tested veteran.

His beady eyes sharpened as in one glance he looked me up and down. "Six foot, are you?"

"Six foot one and a half."

"Guards," he snapped.

No suggestion could have filled me with greater horror. I was not made for cold steel, hand to hand fighting, and all that Duke of Wellington stuff.

"No, not infantry," I parried.

He gave me a stare of sheer hate. I guessed he had been an infantryman himself.

"Well, what?"

"I've just come from overseas," I explained, "and I don't

have any idea what regiments there are."

He grew angrier than ever. "Look here, all the others who come to join up know exactly what they want."

"Couldn't I see a list or something?"

"My God, you're the most difficult man I've ever had in this office." He jerked a document from a drawer in his desk and began to read it or rather shout it aloud. He rattled it off so fast that I could only catch a few regimental titles here and there. "RA, RAOC, RAMC, RASC ... RE, REME ... and so on. He made no attempt to explain what these curious initials might mean. Such information was something else I ought to have known while I was doubtless dodging the column abroad.

Breathless, he reached the end of his list, flung the booklet down onto his desk. "Well?" he glared.

I could see I had no chance. It was not to be a rational war for me; from the very first it was a madhouse. I might as well have stuck a pin in the list.

"Well, which is it to be?"

"I'll take the first on that list," I answered with calculated indifference.

"RA?"

"Royal Artillery," I translated. As a matter of fact that was the only set of initials I'd been able to recognise. My father had been in the Artillery in the first World War, and had come back unscathed. I'd gained from him the comforting notion that guns must be some distance back from the front line. The heavier the gun the further back. I was wondering whether I could ask my recruiter how to get into something really heavy. But he was already handing me a printed application form.

"Right," the little man said, "sign here." As I signed he dug into his pocket and passed me a grubby silver coin, the traditional king's shilling that volunteers received to seal their bargain.

"Report here, 0900 hours tomorrow," he sneered.

Depressed and humiliated, I wandered round the drab wartime streets, trying to find my bearings. In the end I sat on a bench in one of London's squares and waited for the nearest pub to open. I understood how George the Mexican must have felt as we voyaged through the grim Atlantic waters.

Sitting alone amid the noise and cheer of the pub as it began filling, I tried to accustom myself to the strange new atmosphere of wartime London. In the dim dark and the chatter of the bar a young girl accompanied by an older woman came over to my table.

"Mind if we sit down?" she asked. I said I didn't mind at all.

She looked at me sharply. "You American?" I denied it. "Canadian then?" I shook my head. We were smiling at each other, as young people do, so easily and naturally. "But you've got an American accent."

She herself had a warm Cockney accent, and I liked it. It was homely and it had a sense of place with which I could identify. You knew exactly where you were with this voice. Spontaneous and natural, there was a blend of worldliness and innocence in it, as if the innocence was a bubbling spring and the worldliness a rock which the spring could easily flow around. I told the girl and her companion the story of my voyage back from the States and of my enlistment that afternoon as 'an overseas volunteer'.

"You *volunteered*?" the older one said, with disbelief. Then, as if it was too much for her, she got up and went to the loo. "You're crazy," the younger one smiled. I told her about the blotchy-faced captain.

"Oh my Gawd," she exclaimed, "you really want your head examined." Her voice was warm and comforting, though. "Let's go out," she said suddenly, "before my friend comes back."

We rose hastily and hurried to the door, pushing our way through a thick curtain which masked the lights of the saloon from the darkness of the street and at the same time held back the silence of the night from the noise and jollity of the pub.

Outside, night had fallen, and pub, houses, shops, the entire street, were blacked out. There was no moon, and it was not easy to distinguish between the pavement and the road. So we hung on to each other; her arm was warm, so was her waist as I slid my arm around it. A couple of steps from the pub and we were lost in pitch black.

"You'll get used to it," she encouraged. "Anyway I know this part like the back of me hand."

She led me across the road to the opposite pavement, we passed a couple of apartment blocks, then she drew me into a deep shop doorway.

As I held her against the shop door, the calm softness of the night blanketed out the whole world around us; there was no war, no angry-voiced captain, no doubts or anxieties, only the firmness of one flesh meeting the softness of another's. She took her arms from round my neck, pulled up her skirt front, slipped her arms back to draw me even closer. "Quick," she said, "before anyone comes."

She was passing on her love like a lucky charm. It was better than any bishop's blessing. It was like being sent off to war with a wave and a salute.

We didn't ask each other's names. It was pointless when tomorrow at 0900 hours I would be gobbled up by the army and sped away to oblivion of one sort or another. She knew better than I did that you could not expect to defeat the monstrous regimentation of war by promises, pledges, or vows. All you could do was to give some warmth, some love, some solace here and now.

Next came six weeks of square-bashing at Maryhill Barracks in Glasgow. It was mid-October, the Scottish winds whistled chilly across the parade ground. Everywhere was dank and grey. The barrack buildings were dilapidated, condemned as unfit since the end of World War I. Day after day of square bashing, evening after pointless evening of blanco-ing, brasso-ing, boot blacking and mindless polishing—it all seemed a long way from my original naive idea of helping to win the war by giving up my college lectureship and nobly volunteering against everyone's good advice.

Maryhill was just the place and October just the month for sergeants to pile misery upon their young recruits. In the second week of our training one eighteen year old squaddie found a use for his newly issued army rifle and blew his brains out. It made quite a mess in the barrack room, and it caused the rest of us a lot of bother. The authorities held an inquest: not so much into the cause of his suicide as to find out how he'd got hold of live ammo. The result for us was added restrictions and extra drill, learning to slow march for his funeral.

Fortunately, there was Gully. Like me, he was older than the others and had a bunk next to mine at the far end of the barrack room. Gully had been an infantry officer somewhere in West Africa, had served in a couple of campaigns, and then in a quieter spell been cashiered over a little matter of some gambling debts which he couldn't meet. Returned home, he re-enlisted in the Artillery. He had a thirst for cards like an alcoholic for drink. I accompanied him, tramping the streets of Glasgow to help him find a bridge club, and when at last we were successful he was pleasantly grateful. "You've saved my sanity, old boy," he said, and in his gratitude to get back to serious card-playing he gave me his copy of *The Screwtape Letters*, a book whose humour we shared and one which helped me survive the darkest days of basic squaddie training.

"What on earth made you volunteer?" Gully asked me one day.

"Politics," I said. "I was one of those pre-war anti-Fascists who talked so much about resisting Hitler. I felt I had to put my service where my mouth had been. I'm fighting Hitler not because he's a German, but because he's a Nazi."

"Left Book Club stuff, eh?" said Gully.

"That's right," I said.

"And pride?" Gully queried. "Too proud to opt out altogether?"

"I had a good job," I said. "I was in the middle of my Ph.D. It wasn't easy. It was a moral choice."

Gully looked at me quizzically. "I *like* the army," he said. "Anyone who doesn't really like the army but joins up all the same, must feel a bit lonely. All that high moral ground—a bit chilly up there, old boy."

He never referred to it again, but afterwards I noted he looked after me with a special sort of indulgent tenderness reserved only for fools and horses. Part of this concern was trying to warn me what to expect. "The sergeants will treat you like dirt, till you begin to feel like dirt—if you let them. It's a simple idea within their heads; first they'll break you, then they'll make you."

"Why should they think they have to break you to do this?" I asked, thinking of the lad whose coffin we had slow-marched to its burial place.

"Only way, old boy. Make you in their image—these boys have been in the *desert*, you know—they'll make you an automaton on parade, so that you're an automaton under fire. Finest fighting man in the world the British soldier. Especially the Scots."

I couldn't be sure when he was being serious and when he was being ironic.

"I thought you officered Africans?" I said.

"That's right. Africans—next best fighting men in the world. Trained by us, you see."

Gully wore a supercilious smile, but I think he meant it all the same.

Mostly he held army officer values at a cool distance. Rank and promotion meant little to him. "It's a matter of luck," he would say coolly, "like getting a gong. It's having the luck to be in the right place at the right time. There's no actual logic about it." Coming from a veteran of the war in distant places the remark, more original then than now, seemed utterly convincing.

Certainly none of my early postings seemed to be 'the right place'. There was a long hard winter in Yorkshire, followed by a tedious spring and summer, as we learned the skills of signalling. We practised morse code till our heads were bursting with wild buzzings. We laid miles of telephone cables with blistered hands. We tore on motorbikes up and down grassy hills and quarry-like sandpits, over the Pennines and down the Snake Pass in ice and freezing cold. Off duty there were local girls in Wakefield we might take for a drink and a cuddle; bus conductresses who wouldn't accept our fares if we were in uniform; waitresses who'd insist on charging for one cake when a tableful of us had owned up to a dozen; warmhearted Yorkshire male civilians, who would invite us off the street to their home (and their astonished wives) for Sunday lunch or a high tea.

I missed Gully. In need of no further training, he'd been shipped post-haste to Burma. Not many card games in the jungle. I never heard of him again. Sparks flying from an anvil and vanishing into space for ever in opposite directions. Relationships that last are not for automata. Wanted: a mate to share the good things with—yesterday, today, tomorrow. Impossible: *carpe diem* should have been the motto on our cap badge. The RA put it more succinctly *Ubique,* sparks everywhere.

In the autumn *ubique* meant OCTU. Wakefield heaths were replaced by Catterick mud, and instead of signalling we found ourselves dragging heavy guns through marsh land specially chosen to bog down in. Heaving a twenty five pounder in thick mud I tore my Achilles tendon. The MO downgraded me to C3, a grade reserved for lunatics, those suffering from syphilis, and (apparently) cripples like me who could not parade in boots.

The tendon didn't heal for months; my intake passed out and I remained in suspended animation. Neither fit nor wounded; neither officer nor yet sent back to the ranks. My luck, which seemed to have played such a scurvy trick, in fact turned providential. When all others of my intake received their postings, they went either to Burmese jungles to fight against the Japs or joined units about to take part in the D-day landings in Normandy. "It's all luck," Gully had foretold—an arbitrary co-ordination of time and place—promotions, medals, dying. Most of the boys who'd gone to OCTU with me would earn one or other of these. As for me, I had a torn tendon, and I was reprieved.

The tendon healed so slowly that I had no hope of starting a new artillery course, so they passed me to the Education Corps. That meant a spell in London during the time of the flying bombs, the V1s and V2s. It also meant that after nearly two years of non-entity Gully's law regarding promotion began to come into effect. One day I was a private. Called on to give a lecture to a forces' unit on life in the USA and—whoops—I suddenly became a sergeant. The sergeant's stripes had barely been sewn on my arm when—whoops again—I was sent down to Wrotham to collect a commission. I was posted as a second lieutenant to Salisbury Plain.

Ready (at last), more or less able, and indubitably willing, I looked forward to notching up some small share in defeating the Nazis and winning the war.

Too late. The war in Europe suddenly, almost shockingly, ceased. Germany surrendered. It was almost all over. Only the Japs were left and, though I did not know it, two atom bombs rather than troops would end it all. It seemed to me typical of all the ironic muddle that nearly two years in the

Army had taught me to expect.

With the end of the war in sight the army had begun to educate its troops in preparation for their ultimate return to civilian life. I was the HQ education officer in the Salisbury Plain region on whom this ambitious programme now devolved.

My colonel was a choleric and war-weary gentleman who was happy to pile upon me vast quantities of work involving ordering, receiving, and distributing books and educational equipment to all the units under his command. A fighting man, Colonel Charman regarded the whole scheme as a bit of politicians' nonsense. As far as he was concerned I could just get on it with it, and he could pretend that it (and I) didn't really exist.

My sole assistant was Sergeant May, another veteran of the war. He had a sharp cynical Cockney awareness, and was willing to work as much or as little as his education officer did. In fact we worked very hard indeed. After about a month I reckon I had passed some sort of test with my sergeant, for he said to me one day: "I suppose you read KRs, sir?"

Since he had added 'sir' to his question, I might have known that it was an important matter on which he was tentatively feeling his ground. KRs, or King's Regulations, were the daily official orders and information sent to all units. Reading of them was supposed to be obligatory; they were the administrative officer's Bible.

"Of course I read KRs," I said loftily.

Behind his glasses I could see his eyebrows lift a little, and his ragged army moustache twitched cheekily. "Then you'll know," he said, "that an education officer must hold the minimum rank of full lieutenant." He held up a copy of the appropriate KR and was pointing to a passage in it. "You should have another pip," said Sergeant May.

As I goggled at him in amazement a sarcastic grin deepened on his face. "You'd better tell the colonel. He'll be pleased to know."

Seeing the colonel about it didn't scare me as much as the sergeant obviously expected. I was too new and too innocent to anticipate that the news might be a bit of a landmine. When I reported the situation to the colonel, a slow purple hue flooded his face, his veins swelled and knotted in his neck.

"By God, young man, I've never had an officer come to me before demanding to be promoted."

"But it's in KRs, sir," I said, pointing to the passage.

"By God, young man, it's damned absurd. Why, you've only just joined the army and here you are jumping up like a jack in the box—"

"Two years, sir."

"Don't interrupt me, young man. As I say you've only just joined the army, and here you are waving King's Regulations at me. It's—it's blackmail. Either I have to recommend your promotion or I shan't have an education officer."

"Yes, sir."

"Very well," he glowered. "But I won't congratulate you. By God, I won't."

All the same I got my two pips. Thank you, Sergeant May. Thank you, dear old Gully.

Then one day not long after, the colonel summoned me to his office. He seemed to be repressing yet another fit of choler. "Telegram from the War House," he barked. "You're to report there immediately." I stared at him, amazed.

"Well, get moving, man."

I told Dickie May to take over the paperwork until I came back. "I don't know what the hell they want," I confided.

"Perhaps they're going to take your extra pip back," he quipped. To him *they* were always capable of anything, especially anything absurd or illogical.

What happened at the War Office was the final triumph of Gully's law. A young brigadier of great charm explained that they wanted to send me to Germany to act as British liaison officer at the US Army HQ at Frankfurt. This liaison was to be with the US equivalent of the Army Education Corps, something the Americans called I&E—Information and Education.

"I expect you wonder how we've come to select *you*," the brigadier grinned.

"I can't imagine," I said. His grin was infectious and I found myself smiling back.

"Modern technology, old boy," he said proudly. "I've got a punched-hole card system here." He indicated a long wooden box with rods running through it—rather like the sort of thing some libraries used to catalogue their books, only with more rods and a bit more Heath Robinson-ish. "You see, we wanted an officer who'd had civilian teaching experience, who'd lived in the States, and who wasn't due to be demobbed for some time. You fitted the bill. We switched on the rods, and out came your card." He tugged at one or two of the controls on his box, but nothing happened. "Damn," he said, "someone's been playing about with the controls."

"What a good idea," I said ambiguously.

"Well, congratulations anyway. Oh, by the way, go along to the tailors before you return to your unit and get a third pip sewn onto you shoulder."

"Oh God," I exclaimed. "My colonel'll have a fit."

"Nonsense, dear chap, leave him to us. Have a night on the town. Tomorrow you can return to your unit and wait there for the documentation to come through for Frankfurt."

"Thank you, sir." I saluted as I took my leave.

He wasn't looking. "Good luck," he said tugging away again at the controls of his modern technology. "I wish I could get this bloody box to work."

III

My orders were to report to Colonel Furze in charge of Army Education, British Army of the Rhine, at Herford in Germany.

"A courtesy call," the Brigadier had said, "en route to US Army HQ, Frankfurt."

Although my assignment was to be in the American Zone, I came nominally under command of BAOR, the British Army of the Rhine. Although my original instructions had come from the War Office and my reports were destined to go there, the reports had to be routed via my commanding officer in BAOR. Nobody envisaged that this would cause any problem.

In BAOR men who had served throughout the war were being demobbed at a commendably bewildering speed. In consequence there was a sudden shortage of officers to replace those being demobbed. Most units had little work to do in these first halcyon days, but the Army Education Corps was unusually stretched and working at full pitch, officially to provide the troops with training for civilian life, or as it was generally regarded, "keeping them occupied until they're demobbed."

The colonel who commanded Army Education Corps considered therefore that of all units in Germany his was most unjustly deprived of officers. The idea that he should now receive an additional officer only to pass on to the Americans seemed like adding insult to injury.

"I'm going to clear this with the War House," he told me.

"You'll stay here in Herford until we get the matter settled."

Unfortunately, the young brigadier who had sent me, together with his punched card box and all the rest of his section at the War Office, seemed to have vanished into the thin mists of demobilisation.

"Can't get any sense from the War House," the colonel said gleefully. "And I can't have you idle. So I'm putting you on normal duties until we hear from them."

His first inspiration was to set me the task of writing an article, which he was later to publish as his own, on the history of Army education. "It'll widen your knowledge," he said.

It was beautiful spring weather. All around us the orchard trees were in blossom and in the little town of Herford the roofs of the houses shone very red. The rough edge of tree-topped hills could be seen a short walk away. Every day when the sun shone—and the sun seemed to shine every day—I was able to sit at my office window and like a prisoner in his cell look down on the lawn beneath.

In the middle of the lawn, keeping the grass short, a goat was tethered to a small, stunted tree. It hated its captivity and plunged like a mad thing until at times the rope seemed likely to break its neck. Occasionally a private in khaki uniform would glide out onto the lawn (strictly forbidden) and pick a bunch of dandelions. Carrying them in his hand, he would calm the plunging white goat and feed it the dandelions as the sun shone overhead in a clear blue sky.

By now the colonel had developed a nice line in tactics. He wouldn't release me to the Americans until the War Office sent him another officer. Telegrams were despatched back and forth, like moves in an angry game of chess. A new brigadier at the War Office immediately caused a stalemate by insisting that I was *not* to undertake 'normal' duties for BAOR. Nevertheless the colonel still held on to me. "Until I get another body out of them," he snapped. "Meanwhile we'll send you on a learning tour of units throughout our Zone in Germany."

"Learning tour?"

"You will learn all you can about our army education system. I'm going to fit you for your job. Make sure you uphold the British standards in the American Zone, eh? *If* you get there," he added in a sort of subdued aside.

Like my previous colonel on Salisbury Plain he was an ex-Indian Army man, and irascible. He was intelligent enough to know when to play act and when to let himself go for real. If he was acting he would cool down and begin to smirk, as much as to say: that was a pretty good performance, don't you think? When he was genuinely angry, though, he was fearsome. I supposed that this ingrained choleric disposition was the result of so many years of service in the exhausting climate of India.

Frankfurt began bombarding us with telegrams. 'Come at once', they said. 'What's the delay?' 'French liaison officers about to arrive.' 'Russki's expected soon. Why no British?' Their anxiety was partly due to the fact that the whole liaison scheme seemed to be heading for the rocks. In fact, neither the French nor the Russians had progressed any further than we had. What disturbed the Americans most was that the American officer who had initiated the scheme was about to be demobbed. I must come at once.

"Not bloody likely," said the colonel, enjoying their discomfiture. "Not till I get a replacement."

He'd send me off on long journeys to units in remote places where I'd spend days on end 'learning' how our own system of army education worked. Each time I returned from one of these visits he would seem taken with amazement.

"Good lord, you back already?"

"Thought there might he some news from War Office, sir."

He'd swear a bit under his breath and call up his adjutant to find somewhere else for me to go. As long as he didn't keep me in HQ but passed me around he reckoned he was safe from burning his fingers with the War Office. My colleagues would laugh whenever I returned from a trip.

"Where've you been this week, hot potato?" they'd ask.

I didn't go much for their potato metaphor. I felt more like the tethered goat, delicately fed on dandelions.

When I told them I'd been to such and such a unit, "Oh that's a right shower," they'd say. And then, inevitably, they'd ask "What are the women like there?"

I'd invent wild tales of some marvellous ATS officers in the unit which I had just visited, and enjoy the green and jealous look that came into their eyes.

The adjutant regularly gave me orders when and where to report on my tours, and issued my travel vouchers etc., but I never got any further instructions than to "learn how things worked" in other units. Nor were those other units given the slightest inkling of why I was visiting them. They were simply told to show me around. So when I arrived in Hanover or Köln or Celle my visitation was regarded uneasily as something of a mystery. I was met and welcomed with unusual respect, dined and wined remarkably well, and the red carpet was laid out for me everywhere. Over cigars and brandy they pumped me cautiously. I could see their unease, but I had nothing more to tell them than that I was there to "learn how things worked." The stonewalling consistency of this reply confirmed their worst suspicions that I had really come to inspect their functioning and to take back a confidential report to HQ.

They were terribly nice to me, and they breathed a sigh of relief when I left.

Each time I returned to HQ, I would dash to the office to enquire whether there was any news from the War Office. None came. The weeks passed, spring turned into summer. The adjutant was running out of units to send me to. Only Berlin was left.

"Right," the colonel ordered. "Berlin it is. No need to hurry back."

IV

Wherever I went in Germany, despatched by my intransigent colonel on one tour after another, I was forced to face the devastating effects of war. Especially travelling by rail.

Coaches, engines, goods trucks by the thousand—shot up, bombed, overturned—littered the railway sidings. Every river had its wrecked bridges. Whole towns seemed uninhabitable, yet people continued to inhabit them. Entire cities—Dortmund, Duisberg, and those famous railway yards at Hamm—lay smashed to rubble. Hardly a building had even one gaunt and lonely wall raised skywards.

It was the same as I journeyed to Berlin. We passed miles and miles of heath and seemingly endless stretches of ox-tilled agricultural land in between towns; the towns themselves were shattered. Living amid the devastation a dazed population treated us as a new master-race who had superseded their former masters. Along the railway lines children scrambled and fought for buns and apples thrown to them by the allied soldiers in passing trains. Children were everywhere, and wizened old people; but young men between the ages of eighteen and thirty had disappeared. In the streets old men dived and scrambled for fag-ends idly thrown into the gutter, and from darkened doorways girls would slip out to offer themselves for a handful of cigarettes. The first time this happened was unnerving. Yet within days one became accustomed to the experience and accepted it as an inescapable fact of post-war life.

It seemed the same in Berlin, only worse.

It was in Berlin that I visited the home of the countess. She and her three daughters lived in a gracious old house in the Charlottenberg district of Berlin. Although the building was grand enough by ordinary standards, it clearly was not large enough for all their possessions. Beautiful tapestries lined the walls, paintings were hung so close as to give the impression of a provincial art gallery; silverware stood proudly on the fine tables and carved sideboards of another age.

Outside, the garden had become neglected and quaintly overgrown; and the house itself had a sort of makeshift air, as though it was merely a temporary lodging place, an overnight stop in a day's hard travelling from one castle in the past to another that lay ahead. Meanwhile the family stretched out its tentacles to obtain what security and grip on life it could, and the widowed countess occupied herself in re-organising its fortunes through her daughters. She had obtained for them suitably genteel occupations in the only rewarding sphere available to aristocratic and educated young ladies in such uncertain times; that is, as civilian employees attached to the British military officialdom. One as a high ranking officer's secretary, one as an interpreter, and Beate, the youngest, as an assistant in the British Forces library.

After a leisurely lunch I had gone to the library one sunny afternoon as part of my mysterious and time-filling inspection act. In order to give the impression of having some realistic purpose in view, I produced a short list of books whose availability I wished to check, and asked for a copy of Graham Greene's *The Power and the Glory* and TS Eliot's *Collected Poems*. A young Nordic-looking assistant, I doubt if she was twenty, fetched them for me.

Absorbed in Greene's Mexico and the drama of his whiskey-sodden priest I became unaware of time and circumstance. It was with a mild irritation that some time later

I was disturbed in an otherwise still room by the sound of whispered consultation going on between the pretty young assistant and her colleague.

It was obvious from their reaction when I looked up that they were discussing me. She was not disconcerted when she saw me look up, but smiled politely and came over to my table. She was tall, with a lissome figure, and dressed simply in the plain style that had once been the fashion with the Hitler Maidens, with her hair in a long thick blonde plait.

"He is a good writer," she said, standing beside me. I could almost feel the mysterious tingle of youth pass between us. "But a little bit depressing, yes?"

I marvelled at her self-assurance; no other German—no other German at all—had spoken to me with such easy confidence. She was quite free of the vanquished-to-victor tone, and spoke as one peer to another.

"It is time now for me to close the library."

I looked around and was aware that everyone else had gone.

"Perhaps I could issue the book on loan, Herr Captain, if you wish to continue your reading?"

"Thank you," I said, "but I have time to spare and can come again."

As she replaced the book on the shelves I added, "I'm new to Berlin, so to discover a library so pleasant—and so well-stocked—is quite a find."

"It is here for the British forces," she said with a little shrug. "To the victors the spoils, is not that so?"

Her English was excellent, an almost perfect accent. We continued talking: nothing much, the usual banalities beneath which the real signals seek to make contact. Then, blushing slightly, she asked whether as I was new to Berlin and perhaps lonely for civilian company, I would like to come and spend the afternoon with her and her family on Sunday. I said I'd be delighted. She gave me her card, with the Charlottenberg address on it.

"Oh, by the way," she said as we were leaving, after locking up the library, "don't forget to bring Mama a little present, will you? All the officers who come to visit my sisters always bring a present. You know—wine, or cigarettes or chocolate or coffee. You won't forget, will you? Mama would be so hurt. Poor Mama, it is very hard for her, you know, this kind of life ... I shall be expecting you."

Back at the mess I made some discreet enquiries. Everyone there seemed to know the countess and her family.

"Oh, yes," the colonel assured me, "good old family. No harm in visiting them, my boy. Very pro-British, you know."

And a redheaded major, overhearing, added, "But don't forget to take the old lady a present. Sticklers for etiquette and all that."

Whereupon Captain McGowan gave me a wink and taking me aside whispered in his cynical way, "And the girls. They want presents too. But if you hope to get anywhere with them, you're wasting your time, old chap."

Nevertheless, I was fascinated by the family name and flattered by Beate's interest, so on Sunday I loaded myself with suitable small gifts and set off through the rubble-strewn streets lined by fire-gutted skeletons of empty houses. Burnt-out tanks still stood, like museum exhibits, by the roadside. Parts of hideous bronze statues of Kaiser Wilhelm I lay twisted grotesquely on the pavements. Iron lamp standards sprawled where they had fallen. Even the rose trees in the Tiergarten had been cut down and filched for firewood. It was a hard, bitter year for the Germans.

The old doorbell creaked as I tugged it, and a dull cracked metallic sound echoed somewhere inside. Creepers trailed drunkenly round the front of the house and over the garden trellis.

At the door Beate welcomed me with warm radiance. "Have you remembered your present for mother?" she asked conspiratorially. "And my two sisters, have you a present for them? And, of course, you have saved something—just a little—for Beate, yes?"

The presents were taken by Beate, with the solemnity of a collection in church, into a gloomy, panelled library, and carefully deposited on the heavy writing table which stood under the window like an altar. Everything was as neat and orderly as the leather-bound books that packed the library shelves.

The family themselves were equally impressive, even the girls had a stately manner. The mother, tall and most stately of them all, was sombrely dressed. Perhaps she was mourning her late husband, perhaps the family fortunes. She greeted me graciously, made a few tactful enquiries about my stay in Germany and, finding that I was comparatively new to the country, began to enlighten me as to the general situation. The British were wonderful, of course; they played cricket, which was clearly a game for gentlemen. And the girls had had an English governess, hence their very good accent. Moreover, the British had one great advantage—they weren't Americans. Americans were very loud and coarse and given overmuch to such impractical ideas as equality and democracy in all things. But the unspeakable monsters were the Russians. They were unshaven, and they raped women; in addition they were Communists.

With tactful restraint the mother merely hinted at the family's East German estates, which the Russians had confiscated. She thought the British and the German people were born for friendship with one another. Only that madman Adolf Hitler had failed to see this and to realise that Britain and Germany side by side could have dealt with Russia. And even yet still could. Meanwhile what could she do but show her sympathy for the British at Hitler's foolish and vulgar treatment of them, by inviting His Majesty's officers to tea each Sunday and sending her girls to work in a humble capacity in HM Forces as civilian clerical assistants. Because, after all, a British officer was also a gentleman, and this is what had been wrong with Hitler; he had been no gentleman. Look how he had slighted the officer corps to which her late and much lamented husband had belonged.

In the course of this exposition various fellow officers and gentlemen kept arriving with packages, larger or smaller, which had to be put in their proper places on the table. We sat awkwardly on heavy straight-backed chairs, a gradually increasing number of us, with three girls and Mama. Later, from a splendid silver teapot Mama poured tea, a custom, she told us, that she had instituted specially for the British.

"I think you said you are new to Germany," Mama said turning to me, for it was now my turn to take part in the conversation.

I mentioned that I had been acquainted with many Germans before coming to Germany—refugees.

"Oh, Jews," said Mama, striking a nice note of balance betwen scorn and sorrow, "they are not *real* Germans."

"Of course," put in Beate who had been watching my face, "we don't approve of what Hitler did to the Jews. But all the same it is possible to understand his reasons."

"Which is more than one can say for many of his actions," piped a young lieutenant with curly blond hair and a high-pitched voice.

Mama raised her hands expressively. "Lieber Gott, the man was maniac. To make war with Britain and then to attack Russia afterwards ... we should have made friends with Chamberlain, then attacked Russia together. Everyone knew that, my husband knew that, the Officer Corps all knew that... but that lunatic, what harm has he done to our Fatherland!"

There was a sudden gabble about political strategy and military strategy. The words Chamberlain—Hitler—the Russians—kept cropping up.

Stung by their comments, I turned to Beate and, remembering her dress at the library, I said to her, "Tell me, were you ever enrolled in the Hitler Maidens?"

The words fell in—or perhaps themselves created—a sudden deathly hush in the previously animated conversation.

Beate blushed. "For a short time, I think, I belonged. For much of the war I was too young. But my sisters ..."

Her mother gave her an angry glance. The older sisters were flung into a flutter of excuses and exculpations. "It was not possible to avoid—All girls of a certain age were made to enrol—We had to do it but we did not like."

Mama broke the flurry of explanations, as she put her china teacup and saucer down firmly on the table and said in quiet but steely tones: "We also were in prison under Herr Hitler, you must remember."

An awkward silence fell on us all.

"And now," said Mama, "I am feeling a little tired. I think that my migraine returns, so I will leave you to be entertained by my daughters while I go to lie down."

She moved elegantly and with a kind of professional graciousness as she left us. But as the door closed behind her, the atmosphere suddenly relaxed. The three daughters began to giggle and from young ladies became transformed into girls. The officers loosened their upright postures on the carved oak chairs, and began to lean their bodies and lounge their limbs like relaxed young athletes.

"Cigarette?" I asked Beate, opening my cigarette case.

"Danke schön."

I took one myself and fumbled for my lighter. I flicked the switch and held the lighter towards her. But Beate had already turned away, her hand creeping out of the pocket into which she had slipped the cigarette. She was talking to my neighbour, the blond lieutenant. I saw him take a crumpled packet of Players from his pocket and lift it up long enough for Beate to see it. He was a very young boy, not much older than Beate, and it was obvious he was quite gone on her.

Beate gave a quick nervous look around the room.

"Zehn Zigaretten," he stressed. I knew what he meant: ten cigarettes were worth a lot on the black market.

"Nur ein Kuss," Beate whispered.

In a few moments she took his hand and led him quietly out to the garden.

It seemed a good moment for me to slip away too. There were four or five officers grouped around the two remaining girls. One of the officers produced a bottle of champagne. He had been concealing it, he said, until after the countess had retired ... I left them, as they laughed and thought how well they were getting on with one another.

Creeping out along the hall corridor, I passed the half-opened door of the library, and through the crack I caught a glimpse of the countess, sitting very erect, neatly sorting the day's presents into well-ordered piles

Her migraine seemed to be much better.

"You're just jealous, old chap," said my friend Captain Mc-Gowan, as we sat knocking back our whiskies in the magnificent, vast and almost empty Officers' Club. "You're jealous of that young fool in the garden. I could have told you that you wouldn't get anywhere with Beate."

"It's not that, it's their bloody politics that get me. They'll have us in a war with Russia in no time."

"Don't you believe it, old chap, our blokes aren't that daft."

As we sat there, trying to warm our spirits with another nip of whiskey, there was a rumble outside as though an army was passing through.

"Hey," somebody called from the window, "it's the Russkis."

We all made our way, drinks in hand, to the large window which looked out on the highway. There was a long procession of Russian troops and equipment passing through the street. The men looked grubby in their grey uniforms, but they had the same wild look as the Russian sentries who so effectively halted visitors to the death bunker of Hitler in the grounds of the Reichs-Chancellerei, tommy guns at the ready. Their fierceness was increased perhaps because their features were an unfamiliar Mongolian; and they did not smile or wave. There was some jeering from the Germans in the street.

"Unshaven lot," said the major. "Slovenly. Our chaps would make mincemeat of them in no time."

"Hear, hear," said another voice. "Sub-human, the apemen of Siberia."

"If Hitler hadn't been such a blasted fool," said a third, "he'd have finished that lot off properly."

"You see what I mean," I whispered to Mac as we returned to our seats at the bar. We sat there for a while, each silent with his thoughts. I felt as though the cold hand of World War 3 was already stretching out to tap my shoulder.

"Hello, young fellow," said the colonel. Behind the bar the German waiter sprang to attention and clicked his heels smartly. "Well, how did you get on at tea with the countess? Rather a grand old lady, isn't she? Distinguished family, the right sort, eh?"

"And," added the major obsequiously behind him, "frightfully pro-British. When you see those fellows outside you know who your real allies are, by God."

My fit of cold shudders returned and with it a kind of nightmare vision in which there were German children begging for food to be thrown from passing trains; Mongol troops waving tommy guns madly; and presiding over it all a lean, aristocratic old lady, at whose feet were laid, like wreaths at a monument, little parcels of food from British officers and gentlemen. I had a dull and hopeless feeling as though the war were not really over, but only just beginning.

These thoughts had little time to mature, for suddenly I received a phone call from Herford to return at once. A War Office rocket had landed on the colonel's desk. I was to travel by jeep from Herford to US Army HQ, Frankfurt. Pronto. I couldn't believe my luck. At last I was going to be able to get on with the job I was chosen for.

V

Head of the inter-allied section of the I&E unit in Frankfurt was sharp, amiable, bespectacled US Major Haynes.

"Hey!" he shouted joyfully across the office as he was sorting his morning mail. "We've got a countryman of yours coming to talk to the troops on the first of next month."

I had been in Hoechst, a suburb of Frankfurt, with the American I&E unit for just two weeks. I was a solitary Brit and it felt strange. I could have done with some back-up—a typist, car, and a clerical worker, someone like Sergeant May. All I got from the Americans was friendliness and obstacles. I hadn't yet come to terms with the relaxed, apparently carefree, methods of the major's office, the general muddle saved by last minute improvisations and disregard of protocol. It was making me feel out of place and prickly. And this latest bombshell seemed to embody everything that was making me feel like a cat on broken glass.

"What the hell's going on?" I exclaimed. "*I'm* the one who's supposed to arrange the British representation here. Remember?"

The major hardly heard me, he was so excited at his news. He bounded over to my desk, waving his document. His eyes glinted and blinked happily through his gold-rimmed spectacles; they were beginning to slip down his nose. "Our first speaker from overseas," he exulted.

"Listen," I said, getting up. "It looks like you don't need a liaison officer, I'm here just for the shop window show. Trawl up your own speakers, major, as much as you like, but leave the Brits for me."

The major was, I really believe, genuinely surprised at my reaction. He swallowed hard, and began rapidly to explain that this was a surprise to him too; certainly there was no calculated intention to go behind my back. "Some weeks ago," he argued, "before you came, I mentioned to a guy from the US Embassy in London that we needed a speaker. The Embassy must've fixed it up. Maybe they met this guy at a dinner party or sump'n."

He looked at me pleadingly, like a naughty boy, crestfallen at my bursting of his bubble of good news. He had just about lived for this moment—his personal D-day launch for the I&E liaison programme.

"It's some labour boss," he said, "named Elvin. Do you know him?"

"Never heard of him," I said, with grim satisfaction.

"It's a commitment," pleaded the major. "Via the Embassy. That means it's got to be honoured."

He looked at my unenthusiastic face. "What's wrong with that?" he pressed. "We're here to get speakers and this guy's a speaker, isn't he? We're here to build up Anglo-American relations and that's sure as hell what this visit will be doing, won't it?"

Since we had a Labour Government in Britain at that time, it occurred to me that a trade union leader might not be a bad lead-in to a programme for US forces on Britain Today. Better than twaddle about aristocratic homes and royal families which the tourist trade were likely to send me. But who was this fellow Elvin?

I looked him up in a reference book in the library. 'Conscientious objector in World War I', his entry read. 'In 1928 in the thick of the General Strike. General Secretary of one of the white collar unions. Former Chairman of the Trades

Union Congress'. It was promising. 'Jailed nine times for asserting the right of free speech'—that was the bit that really cheered me. One could do something with that.

I pointed out to the major with vengeful pleasure that our lecturer was probably a militant left-wing unionist and would use his visit to convert all the American troops into revolutionary socialists before his fortnight's tour was done. The major paled a little.

"No politics, there must be no politics in our programme. We must make that clear. I think I'd better send him a cable."

"Go ahead," I said. "After all, he's your man, not mine."

"Nine times jailed. Wow! I'm surprised at our Embassy sending out a man with his extreme political views. Trade unionism and politics—are you sure that's his subject?"

"He's a union leader, so what else is he going to talk on, if he's not going to talk on trade unionism? And it's bound to be militant left-wing stuff. You can tell that from his record."

"I'll send the Embassy a cable that he's got to make it non-political. Nothing that will stir up the troops."

The arrangements were the major's; my job was to develop publicity for the visit. Posters in offices and messes, in the Red Cross canteens and in the Post Exchange shops advertised the forthcoming appearance of the leading militant of the British Labour movement. 'Free speech Elvin. NINE TIMES JAILED', I captioned. 'The man they couldn't gag'.

The major got more and more jittery and began sending off cables in all directions.

It was a dull, cloudy, sticky sort of day when our lecturer arrived. I was at the airport with the major to meet him. He came out of the plane limping: a tall, thin, wrinkled, determined-looking old man with a gammy leg.

Was it true, I asked as we rode in the jeep to the I&E office, about his having been at one time imprisoned by the British authorities?

"Certainly. Nine times," he said with some pride. Then he added almost apologetically, "but that was when I was a very young man."

"Defending the right of free speech?"

"Yes, indeed. It was at the Bull Ring in Birmingham where open-air meetings had traditionally been permitted."

"Was that in connection with the General Strike?"

"Oh, dear me, no. It was in the course of a series of lectures I was undertaking for the temperance movement."

I don't think the major had been listening, because he turned to our guest and said "The first thing we must do is fix you up with a ration card and a PX card."

"What is that?" enquired Britain's leading militant teetotaller.

"A ration card entitles you to eat in the mess. Also to a liquor allowance."

"That won't be necessary," I whispered, "he's tee-total."

The major goggled in astonishment. He had heard about rationing in Britain and with natural benevolence he'd very much wanted to dispense his goodies. They were, he reckoned, a powerful illustration of the American way of life.

"OK, he's still entitled to a card," he argued. "Of course, if he prefers not to use it we could just keep it in my desk." He gave me a wink, then leaning across me and turning to our guest he went on. "There's one other card which entitles you to use the PX."

"And what is the PX?"

"PX—Post Exchange—that's a typical American name for army stores. I guess you don't have anything like that in your country. It means while you're over here you can buy goods of various kinds, say toothpaste, soap, sweets, wrist watches, pyjamas, the lot. Most anything you fancy is stocked in the PX. At about half the civilian prices. Maybe you'd like to take a couple of wrist watches back, real cheap, to sell in the UK?"

The old man looked shocked.

"Never mind, you'll probably see something else you like. Oh yes, I nearly forgot, you're entitled to a carton of cigarettes a week. That's two hundred cigarettes."

"I don't smoke," he protested.

"Sure," the major urged, "but you want to purchase them all the same. So you've got something to trade with on the black market. You can get almost anything on the black market for two hundred cigarettes. How about a nice Leica camera now?"

Elvin drew himself up, as much as one can in a jeep. "I have no intention either of purchasing cigarettes or of taking part in any kind of blackmarket activity. Thank you, I do not wish to see the interior of a PX. In fact I'm rather surprised that you, as a senior officer, have made these suggestions to me."

We fixed him up quickly in his hotel and got back to the office to think things over.

"Say, are all Englishmen like him?" asked the major, blinking at me through his thick spectacles. "I guess he's nuts. A guy doesn't drink. OK, so that's no reason to waste a good liquor ration. A guy doesn't smoke, so that's no reason not to make use of his cigarettes. Hell, I was only trying to do him a favour."

The first talk was on the following afternoon, to an airforce contingent a few miles out at Wiesbaden.

"What's the audience likely to be, major?" I enquired.

"Full house. Compulsory parade for all troops not engaged on fatigues."

"Compulsory parade? How the hell can we build up good relations if you go and arrange compulsory parades?"

The major shook his head with resigned patience. "Listen, this guy is the first shot in our goodwill campaign. We've got to give it the big build-up, so everybody in HQ knows about the work of our section. This guy may be a nut case but I got plans for him. Yessir, he's gonna address every unit in

Frankfurt this week before we send him off to Berlin. I want every US enlisted man to have heard this guy. And every goddam general. This is our chance for the big breakthrough. Oh boy, if we can just get the generals interested in the work of this section—Wow!"

"And the rest of the talks, are they to be compulsory?"

"Sure," said the major. "You want everyone to hear your countryman, don't you? Besides, there's been so much publicity about his being the leading militant in Britain that everybody wants to see the guy."

It was the hottest day of the summer. When our truck arrived at Wiesbaden we had to help the old man clamber down the back of it. The ride had been over the high-cambered, cobbled German roads and it obviously had shaken him up a bit. He didn't complain, refused to admit that it had been other than a fine ride, and was in a lively and cheerful mood. He was amazed to hear that his audience was to be between five and six hundred men.

"I trust they are all volunteers," he said.

The major didn't hesitate a second. "You've caused a big stir coming out here, you know. It's the first visit any non-American has made and they're all real keen to hear what you have to say to them."

"Amazing, quite amazing. An audience of—five hundred, did you say?—on a beautiful day like this. I should have thought they would want to get out into the countryside on such a day, not listen to an old man's rhetoric."

"Ah, you don't know the American troops," observed the major.

But I did, and I viewed them with alarm. They were drawn up in formation on the tarmacked square outside the large building in which the talk was to take place. The men were scowling darkly and as the hot sun beat down on them looked as enthusiastic as men on their way to prison.

They marched in under the watchful eyes of a single duty

officer and a small squad of NCOs. When the hall filled, I noticed the officer quietly disappearing. And the speaker was left with five hundred and sixty enlisted men. The title of his lecture was 'A History of British Trade Unionism'. He stated that he intended to trace this from medieval times and show the parallels between the medieval guilds and the modern union. He'd an enormous sheaf of typed foolscap in one hand, and with the other he carefully poured himself a glass of water before he began to read from the sheaf.

We heard about the weavers' guild, and the Flemings; we had Chaucer quoted at us. He'd researched it well, and it was deadly boring. We were told of the relations between the master craftsman, the journeyman, and the apprentice. We heard of the Black Death and the Statutes of Labourers 1340-1350. He may or may not have got on to the Peasants' Revolt of 1381. I do not know because at this point we began to have a revolt of our own. It began with a growing murmur among the men. Soon amid the buzz there came some sinister booming sounds, and in a sort of rivalry other jokers started emitting high pitched squeaks. There were bronx cheers and a slow handclap; whole rows of feet now began to stamp the floor. The old boy ploughed on relentlessly, sheaf of foolscap shaking in one hand, the other arm gesturing from time to time. Suddenly he stopped dead in his tracks. There was a big cheer from his audience.

As he held up his hand they quietened to hear his admission of defeat. Waiting until there was a pin-drop silence he said in his steely determined voice, "I've been paid to give you a lecture on the development of British trade unionism. So I'm going to give you this lecture whether you listen to it or not. Every time you stop me you are keeping yourself here that much longer. The quieter you are, the sooner you will get away; the more noise you make the longer you will stay."

Men jumped to their feet shouting, waving fists. I will swear I saw a couple of whiskey flasks appear, waved and passed from hand to mouth. It took the NCOs quite a time to get that lot under control. In the end he got through it right up to modern times and the establishment of the International Labour Office. He sat down amid cheers and boos, and sipped his glass of water. The men had had their lecture and the lecturer had earned his honorarium. Only I was left to contemplate the wreck of Anglo-American relations.

The major had food for thought too. After all, he had arranged for a dozen or so similar lectures to be given, compulsory parades and all, throughout the headquarters area. It was true that next week the speaker would be sent to Berlin, but in the meantime...? The major said nothing as we went home in the truck; he was obviously brooding. When we disembarked, however, he was himself again.

"Well," he said, "that was quite an experience. Yessir, you really roused them that time. I guess that's the first genuine educational experience some of those men have ever had. My, oh my," he said, "wait till you get out to those troops down south, they're really going to love it, all that stuff about the craft guilds and the Flemings. Say, did that Peasants' Revolt really take place in your country?"

"Down south?" he asked, a little bewildered.

"Yeah, way down at the southern end of the Zone. We'll have a truck run you out there in the morning. Maybe you could stop off at Nuremburg on the way and tell them there about the guilds and all that kinda stuff. I reckon it will sure go down great."

"I thought the arrangement was that I should spend the first week at HQ in Frankfurt and the second week in Berlin."

"That's right. Only there's been a little hitch. The negro units down south are kinda interested and have put in a special request for a speaker; so we've had to map out a completely new programme."

"But—"

"Oh, the week in Berlin is OK. That's still on. You can meet some of the big allied chiefs there. Say, we might even try to see if the Russkis could arrange to have you talk to their troops. You see, this is a reciprocal programme. We mustn't just keep it to one nationality. Then the British are sure to want you. Guess the captain could arrange that ..." He winced just a little as he caught my glare.

Our guest stumped off, puzzled but pacified. The moment he was gone, the major grabbed the phone. "Get Nuremburg. Urgent," he demanded.

"Boy" he said to me, still holding the receiver, "we sure have to get rid of that guy. He'll have the troops mutinying and I sure don't want that happening on *our* doorstep."

"Nuremburg?" said the major to the phone. "Listen, I've got a surprise for you. We've got a guy here who's an expert on the British trade union movement. He's quite a speaker. You guys have been asking for some visiting speaker to entertain the troops, that's right, isn't it? Well, he's coming tomorrow. Yes, we're sending him by jeep. Now you look after this guy; he don't drink, and he don't smoke. Make it a compulsory parade? Oh, yes, sure. After all, he's a pretty big guy in his own country ... And by the way, when you've finished with him, make sure that he goes onto one of those outlying units way down south. He so wants to see as much of the country as he can before he goes to Berlin, so you just send him right on to the next unit and make sure he keeps travelling. O.K., it's a pleasure."

As the old boy left us, I tried to tip him off how things stood.

"You mustn't be too upset," I said, "by the way those men behaved yesterday."

"Oh, no," he said, "not at all. I'm used to public speaking, you know. Never show fear of the mob, and never give way to hecklers."

"But I mean those men weren't really expecting a lecture

on English social history. They were expecting something a little lighter, more of an informal discussion about conditions in Britain today."

He looked shocked. "I've put a lot of work into my research since I retired as general secretary of the union. It's very fascinating work, I enjoy sharing it with the men."

"Look," I tried again, "those men are fed up with being in the army, all they want is to get back home, and in the meantime to be entertained to help make the time pass as quickly as possible to when they're demobbed."

He looked at me a little angrily I thought and on his dignity. "That was not the impression I received from the American Embassy. My honorarium is distinctly on the understanding that I give a series of one hour lectures, non-political in content, on the history of British trade unionism from the earliest times to the modern day."

He clambered awkwardly into the jeep, an old man, well over seventy. Ahead of him lay a week's hard travelling in a bouncy vehicle over German roads. Many of them were still bomb-damaged. I could see from the way he grimaced when he had to lift his gammy leg to step up into the jeep that he was having a lot of pain. Still, there he was, setting out; no fuss about the transport, no querying the major's arrangements. He had a mission to carry out, and civilian that he was and ex-conscientious objector, he certainly wasn't going to be the one to fail in his duty.

I saluted him as he set off.

"I sure hope he gets back in one piece," said the major, looking thoughtful. Then he brightened up. "Say," he said, "did you know we had a cable from the Embassy in Moscow? They're sending us a real live Russian speaker next week."

I looked at him with apprehension.

"Oh, he'll be all right," he added,—"he doesn't speak a word of English!"

VI

The I&E inter-allied section must have been about the smallest unit in the entire US Army. In addition to the major and myself, there was just Loot, the major's second in command, and the two civilian typists, Dutch Julie and the old lady.

Solid, placid, heavy, Julie's huge weight seemed to spill over from her typist's chair and fill an entire corner of the office where she worked. It was as though the chair and the table and she were all of a piece, like a suite of furniture. There was no animation in her expression; she seemed to live in a world of massive immobility.

The other typist was the old lady, also Dutch—we never got to know her name—who seemed always to be grumbling either to herself or to Julie. She hated us, the men in the office. It was not surprising; for there were a lot of pretty girls in HQ, who were made a big fuss over by all the officers from high to low, so that no one had any time for a grumbling old lady, however gallant she might have been in the Resistance. The trouble was that our section was the newest and the least important in the whole of HQ. Despite the major's efforts, no one seemed to know of us; our very existence was forgotten or we were confused with other sections. The natural result of our being so humble in the scale of things was that we got the two least attractive typists in the entire American theatre of operations. They grumbled together in deep guttural Dutch; one blonde, wrinkled old lady and one squat, black-haired piece of living furniture.

Disliking us as they did, they took a delight in annoying us in a dozen or more petty ways. They planned their little annoyances and they plotted together in guttural whisperings, glancing at us, as they spoke, out of the corner of their eyes. Although we could sense that they were discussing us, we could not understand them and this made us feel uncomfortable.

"That great fat slob," the major grumbled, "and the old hag. Who the hell picked them for this section I'd like to know!"

Our attempts to say a cheerful 'good morning' or to crack a joke were received coldly, so that one felt there was as much point in saying 'good morning' to a desk or cracking a joke with the filing cabinet. After such a greeting, they would retreat into that conspiratorial desk-to-desk whispering and little sneering giggles and sidelong glances that made us wish we hadn't spoken. They did everything together, the old one and the young one. They ate their sandwiches at lunch time side by side, went to the loo at the same time, came to work together, left together; and (it seemed) hated us men together.

It was an understood arrangement that the old one did the major's work, and that Julie acted for the rest of the section. Of course, it happened with Julie, as it happened with car transport and with most other services, that there was the usual schemozzle about my own eligibility as a British officer for American facilities. The first lot of typing I handed to Julie she handed straight back.

"I work for the Americans," she stated.

I explained that as a British liaison officer I had the same rights and privileges that the American officers possessed. I added what I hoped would be a winning smile.

"I work for the Americans," she said.

I called the major over, and he confirmed my rights.

"I work for the Americans," Julie reiterated, straightening her papers on the table. She got up and set off for the rest room, followed by the old lady.

"She's a lazy, fat slob," said the major. "If I've asked for a replacement for her once I've asked a dozen times. You just keep working on her. She'll come round. I wonder where in the name of God they found these two."

But she didn't come round, and I had to take the matter to the colonel. He was a battle-scarred veteran and I was newly commissioned and very green. I don't think we understood each other very well. I could see that he thought I'd got all huffy about some imagined insult to the Union Jack and King George. Nevertheless, although I sensed that his sympathies were with the Dutch girl, he sent a directive to the major to supply me with typing facilities. But when Julie refused point blank again, with her "I work for the Americans," the major just gave up. The American lieutenant at the next desk grinned—a captain's discomfiture was funny, even though it was an English captain. Thereafter each day the two typists, as soon as they saw me coming in to work, made off for a council of war in the rest room.

I had a long report to send in to the War Office; and I didn't fancy making it out in longhand. I had already sent telegrams asking for a car and chauffeur, because the Americans were being so awkward about transport. I hardly dared admit so early in my posting that I was failing to win their co-operation in the matter of a typist also.

"Try being nice to her," said the major. "You know, send her flowers and that sort of gewgaw that women love. Make her feel wanted. Let her think you're making a pass at her."

I looked at Julie. She was massive, sexless as an oak. Her legs were thick; and even her striking colouring somehow repelled. Her hair was black, her eyes like charcoal. Her fingers were thick stubs; they descended upon the typewriter keys heavily as though they were thumbs. Her work was full of mistakes—wrong letters typed, letters left out, erasures inadequately made. And invariably the paper carried smudgy fingerprints in one or more places. As the major said, heaven knows where they had got her from; she certainly wasn't a professional typist. One doubted whether in fact she had ever typed at all before she started work on this job, whether she hadn't picked it up as she went along, laboriously teaching herself until she had just enough skill to get by.

Julie just sat there, spilling out of her yellow dress, her stumpy fingers deliberately seeking the pinpoint tops of the keys and plunging them downwards with a kind of hate as she did it. The carbon copy was black and smudgy, like her hair. When I looked at her and, looking up, she caught my glance, her white round face with its unattractive freckles would stand its ground solidly and in her black charcoal eyes I could read the triumphant declaration, "I work for the Americans."

The days were slipping by, and I was pretending that I didn't really need a typist. The lieutenant was grinning, the major was sulking, annoyed that my interview with the colonel had brought a directive to him to do something of which he wasn't capable. Julie looked at me with malignant triumph and the old lady seemed openly to sneer.

"Try being nice to her," the major had urged. "Let her think you're making a pass at her."

The major never lacked for an original idea.

Well, why not? Why not take her out to dine, flatter her, and win her over? The thought crossed my brain and then disintegrated, like a meteor plunging to its own destruction. The thought of her giant mass in one of the officers' exclusive dining places or on the floor of the Castle Kronberg ballroom or anywhere but spilling out of the office typing chair seemed quite impossible. Conversation? There was nothing for us to talk about. Pleasure? There was none to be had. Nor could I ever hope to find her alone without the old dreadnought alongside. She clung to Julie as a limpet to a rock, making all friendly intercourse impossible.

Then one day Julie happened to be alone in the office at lunch-time. The old lady had gone off to get her liquor ration, Julie for some reason remaining behind. I had been out all morning, and when I came in the office was empty except for Julie eating her sandwiches and biscuits for lunch. They looked dry and crumbly. The words came out, I don't know how: "Why not come out to dine with me tonight and have a really decent meal?"

Julie looked up at me imperturbably, with an almost deadening placidity. She didn't look pleased, she didn't look displeased, she looked her normal dull self. "All right," she said, and went on chewing.

"I'll call for you about seven. Where shall I pick you up?"

She didn't reply right away, but ultimately mumbled an address and paid no more attention to me. I thought to myself bitterly, I suppose she thinks she might as well have a night out at my expense, dinner, champagne and dancing at the Castle; and all the while she'll be thinking what a sucker I am. I wished I hadn't asked. I still didn't know how the invitation had slipped out like that, like some dreadful faux pas made in a crowded room.

I crept out of the office, unable to bear being with her any longer, as she continued slowly munching her way through her little bag of rations. I stayed away from the office all afternoon, so that I would not have to contemplate her massive figure and feel the atmosphere of deadness that seemed to exude from her. That greasy black hair, that solemn face and that yellow dress were unchangeable, day in, day out; and I felt I needed a long rest before I tackled them in the semi-romantic light of evening.

I arrived at her billet exactly as the clock struck seven. Julie let me in. Her room was small and dingy, the furniture old-fashioned. She was dressed to go out, in flaming red. It was the only time I saw her dressed in a colour other than yellow. The black hair was neatly brushed and shone with a brilliant sheen; the black eyes that looked at me no longer smouldered with hate. She had not spoken a word, nor had I, since I had rung the doorbell. Her face was as expressionless as ever, but her eyes were warm and wonderfully soft. Her massive body seemed to tingle with pent-up sexuality.

As she slipped her arms round my waist, I felt a wildness, strength and an agility which amazed me. She was as supple as a lioness, her vastness no longer solid but like the vastness of the summer sea. We seemed to swim together in a wide, wide lagoon; and after, as we lay exhausted on the warm, yellow sands, her black eyes were soft as pools of clear water. We forgot about dinner and lay there until the early hours of morning without the need to say a word—about food or drink, or love, or even typing.

Three or four hours later she was in the office, in her yellow dress, spilling over from her typist's chair; placid, untidy— and unperturbed. When I came in, I gathered up my accumulated typing work and took it to her with new confidence.

As she looked up at me I searched for the hint of a smile. Her face was impassive. Slowly and heavily she said, "I work for the Americans."

VII

The experience—or, as one might say—the experiment with Julie made me realise more than ever my own isolation. The Americans had even billeted me in the Polish compound, to which they happily consigned all non-Americans, together with some of their own more dubious civilian characters.

Night after night a Polish sentry sauntered wearily along the street, passing at helmet level the open window of my billet. This he did at regular hourly intervals. Nothing ever happened on his patrol. He was bored out of his mind.

On this particular night my neighbour Johnny, an American civilian whose exact function I never discovered, something to do with the Control Commission for Germany, had his radio on AFN at full blast. His girlfriend, whoever she was that night, was performing the usual routine, frying Johnny his steak and onions in the communal kitchen across the hall. After they had eaten the steak and onions, they would make love. There was a thin partition wall between his room and mine, and I couldn't make up my mind whether to endure hearing their love-noises before or after I went to bed. Still, I might fall asleep. So I undressed just about the time, I imagine, when Johnny was lashing into his blackmarket steak. He had travelled three hundred kilometres to get that cow; I forget how many cigarettes it cost him, or for how many dollars he sold it, after taking a meal from the carcass for himself and his girlfriend for the night.

"Hell," he'd say, "I ain't doing no harm. All I want is to make some dough quick and get back home. I'd do just the same if I was back home, wouldn't I? I knew some guys once that switched a railroad car into a siding, loaded with gasoline, and siphoned it off during the Battle of the Ardennes. Now that's what I call real blackmarketing."

I didn't envy Johnny the trouble he went to on his blackmarketing deals, or the dollars he'd notched up in cashing in on the post-war shortages in occupied Germany. I had a moral aversion to black-marketing, couldn't see how we could ever get the German people back on their feet again if we shut our eyes and let this modern form of looting flourish. Not having done much to win the war, I felt maybe I had a special duty to help win the peace. All the same I had to recognise that Johnny's choice to black market was his affair, just as my refusal to do so was mine, and I accepted that it was his way of dealing with the boredom and alienation which came from serving in an army of occupation.

Johnny had gained himself a reputation among the local girls as one who rewarded them well—with cigarettes—if they caught his fancy. Dressed in their gala outfits from happier times, the frauleins would stroll by his window like fashion models on a catwalk. Johnny had a policy to cope with this demand. It worked out equitably: never the same girl twice.

I discovered this on my first night when one apparently turned up for steak and onions a second time. Johnny was furious with her and I could hear every sound of the scuffle as he started to throw her out. "Out," he was shouting, "Don't you ever come back here." I opened my door as he was dragging her through the hall outside. He stopped and grinned at me.

"Hi," he growled, "I wondered who'd be filling that room. Do you speak English?"

"Nothing else."

"Last guy was a Polack. Now this crazy dame wants me to make love to her. Here, why don't you take her? Give her a drink and some cigarettes, and she's yours. OK, Lieselotte?"

"OK, Johnny," said Lieselotte, turning immediately to me. "You British? I like the British better than the Americans. Americans are gangsters, like Johnny."

"Enjoy yourself," grinned Johnny. "I can't say I rate her much."

"Ja," said Lieselotte, grabbing my arm, "I like British men, they are so handsome; and how tall! Very sexy, not like damn Yankees."

That was how I met Johnny. Drink; black market; sex. These were the options, the three leisure choices of the occupying forces. Johnny aimed to make a small pile out of the black market to take back home to his wife and kids. With him sex was OK but secondary. The more sociable but less enterprising lads enjoyed the cutprice booze and the camaraderie of getting blotto with their mates.

Lieselotte's blatancy didn't appeal to me: I gave her a drink and some cigarettes and sent her away, unemployed, so to say. She didn't mind as long as she'd got her cigarette quota.

All the same, after some weeks of outnumbered struggle with the Americans in their I & E madhouse by day and the nightly experience of Johnny enjoying the by-product of his black marketing jaunts, I began quite desperately to feel a need for the relaxation and stimulation of human and feminine companionship.

So, on this particular close and sultry summer night I undressed slowly, wishing Johnny would finish his steak and onions, make love to the girl, and let me relax and fall asleep in my solitary bed. As I undressed slowly and deliberately, trying to give Johnny and his girl plenty of time, I began to wish that I too had someone to prepare me steak and onions. Even Lieselotte. The trouble with having to listen to the noises from next door was that they gave such proof of

Johnny's gold-medal capacity for love-making. I began to hope for the silence that would indicate failure. Every success that Johnny achieved emphasised my own isolation, so that I began to hate his ruthless efficiency and the crazy rules he had invented for his entertainment.

I got into my hard and narrow bed and turned my face to the faded roses of the wallpaper, listened for a moment or two, then switched off the bedside lamp. The window was open; the thin lace curtains hardly rippled. It was a sweating sort of night. If I had opened the door of my room, maybe I could have got some sort of through-draught, but the door opened into the hall of the big apartment house, and there was usually somebody coming in late, going up the stairs to the rooms above. All I could think of was Johnny and his German girls with their round lovely breasts.

Outside, the Polish sentry slouched past more to relieve his boredom than from any sense of duty. Maybe at the other end of his beat something would turn up. Sometimes the sentries fired off their rifles to amuse themselves by scaring the German civilians; perhaps they would spot a youth slinking back from an alley rendezvous with his girl, or from a night on the town, or from a blackmarket deal. Cows for cigarettes, nylons for coffee, marks for dollars, the Germans had the same diversions as us. Only sometimes the Poles fired a few shots at them just for the hell of it.

Tonight was quiet. No shots. No scuffles. Johnny too was quiet, except he had begun to snore a bit; the fraulein was still, like a mountain river that has long ago reached the alluvial plain. The whole house, the street, the night itself, was at peace and sleeping.

What disturbed my slumber was a vague sense of someone clambering through the window, quietly and gently and without haste. The moon must have been full, because the moonlight broke the utter darkness of the room and made it a shadowy gloom. Silhouetted against the window, the girl who was entering looked as beautiful as a dream. It was so pleasant a dream that I didn't want to press the switch of the bedside lamp, lest the image might fade and be dispelled.

Once, waking in hospital after an operation, I saw a blonde madonna leaning towards me with golden curls tumbling from her cap, her eyes warm with love, her lips moist. I remember floating up towards her; the next moment I was out like a candle. I never recognised her again, but research proved she must have been one of the two middle-aged sisters, very sensible, very kind—and very plain. I knew it would happen like that again, so my fingers closed reluctantly on the switch and squeezed.

The flash of light was like the kick of a rearing horse. I hardly dared look. She was still there—black hair, grey eyes, and a black evening dress which gave her an air of remarkable elegance for one who had just climbed through a window.

"I'm sorry to be in your room," she said. "I didn't mean to waken you." A drift of perfume came with the voice. "It is very embarrassing," she added, looking at me with appealing eyes. "I would like a cigarette, then I can explain better perhaps."

The flame of my lighter flickered, and for a moment the grey eyes seemed all green. "May I sit down? On your bed?"

She was looking at me, calm and tender; once again I was floating upwards. All seemed as sweet as the picking of buttercups in a meadow or the ringing of cathedral bells.

"And perhaps," she prompted, "I might have a drink?"

I stirred out of bed without actually touching her—it was close enough to be a miracle—neither the soft, round curve of her breasts nor the long, tight line of her thigh.

"You have a very small room. Do the Americans always give British officers such a small room?"

I had a bottle of Spanish cognac in my hand and was reaching for two glasses. I poured the brandy into a couple of tumblers. It was strong, rough stuff. Tonight it tasted as though it had got a kicking embryonic life within it.

I took a grip on myself. After all I was an officer in His Majesty's army and how did I know what enemy this nocturnal visitor might be? I put on my best officer voice and said: "Now, suppose you tell me why you are here."

"Prosit," she said, politely evasive.

"Or," and I hated myself saying it, "I shall have to hand you over to the Polish guards."

She looked at me reproachfully. "Yes, I understand. I know you must do that if I cannot explain why I am in the room of a British officer."

There was silence for a moment as she stretched out one nyloned leg a little and took another sip of brandy.

"I came in because—." She chose her time to tell me as the brandy rolled from my tongue into my throat, "because I needed a lavatory."

She sat quite patiently, until I had coughed my windpipe clear.

"The sentry outside was very kind. I said to him, 'Please find me a lavatory,' and he said that there was sure to be one inside."

She was a beautiful actress and she lied entrancingly, looking at me with dove-grey eyes which never wavered. Her explanation was absurd, of course, an excuse thought of in a moment. Yet she sat calm and still and confident. She was as quietly motionless as a tree in the summer sky. Even her breathing seemed suspended.

"The lavatory is outside, in the hall," I offered, nodding my head in that direction.

"Thank you," she said. "I shall find it."

She closed the bedroom door quietly behind her and I heard her switch on the hall light.

Why had she come? It must have been to see Johnny, though she wouldn't want to admit this to me. Or perhaps to see the Polish officer who had been billeted here before me. Or perhaps she thought the room was vacant. Or again she could be on her way to one of the rooms upstairs. Perhaps to escape from someone following her outside ... perhaps to steal ... perhaps in league with the Polish sentry... who knows? ... And why should I care? A ripe apple drops at your feet from a tree: you pick it up. If it looks good or you are hungry, you eat it—no questions. Yet I had let her go. Would she return? I had given her the choice: she could make her own decision. To creep upstairs to the Polish officers, to go next door to Johnny, to slip out by the front door to the street, or even maybe, I hardly dared hope, she could of her own free will come back through the grey-green door of my room.

I lay back in bed and waited. Everything was so quiet, I could hear the seconds ticking themselves away. I began counting one—two—three— and listening for the front door to open and then the quick clatter of her heels escaping down the street. Or perhaps Johnny's door opening and the sounds of a scuffle. I lit a cigarette and waited. For a long time there was no sound, then the handle turned, the grey-green door seemed to open itself.

"You see," she smiled, "it is as I said. Your door is on the left, the lavatory is on the right. I took the wrong turn in the dark, that is all."

"No good," I said, "you came in by the window."

"OK," she said, settling down in a chair beside my bed. "I will tell you the truth. I am Polish. My father is from Poland, but my mother is English. My father is an engineer, that is why the Nazis brought him to Germany. When the Americans came he worked for them. In a few days we go to the USA. We live in the American compound."

She stretched out her hand and touched my wrist. Pushing up the pyjama sleeve a little and bending over, she inspected my wrist watch.

"It is now half-past three. I have been to a dance. It went on very late, and then it was too late to get a car home. So I began to walk and I have walked a long way. I think I got lost a little. I saw a window open and I climbed in. It was yours. That is all. It is very ordinary."

It was not ordinary in the least. The warm scent of the night, the whiff of her perfume, the mystery of her visit, her calm insouciance were strange, dreamlike. I struggled to maintain my sense of military discipline.

"All right. But now it's half-past three and I think we should get some sleep."

"Yes, " she said submissively.

"So I will put on a dressing gown and show you to the front door and you can then make your own way home to the American compound."

The oval of her face broke like a cracked mirror. "It is too late. And the sentry outside will want to question me."

"Then I shall speak to the sentry and tell him to let you pass."

"But there is also my father. He will be very angry. Because I am so late he will say I am wicked and he will beat me. But if I go in the morning he will already be at work and will not know that I am out all night. Please, I beg you to let me stay here tonight."

"But, fraulein, this is a small room and there is only one bed."

"Then *you* must have it, for you must go to work in the morning, is it not so? So I will sit on the chair and I will not disturb you one little bit all night, nor in the morning."

I said I didn't think the arrangement would work.

"Then I will sleep on the floor. I will be very quiet and lie very still so you can sleep."

I didn't think that would work either.

"Not on the floor?"

"No."

"Nor in the chair?"

"Nor in the chair."

"Then there is only one thing to be done," she sighed,

"though it is a very narrow bed."

She began to slip off her evening dress. Her skin was smooth, her body firm. With one hand she felt for her black handbag. She fumbled in it for a moment, then brought out in her clenched fist something small and soft and silky. A transparent nightie unfolded like a conjuror's trick and floated to full length. In another minute she was in bed.

It was a wonderful dream and it went on and on and lasted all night, right through a deep slumber, until the alarm lever tripped its hammer at eight o'clock in the morning.

I opened my eyes, she was not there. Without her the room no longer seemed touched by the play of impudent magic, but bare and drab as it always was. No trace of her perfume lingered in the air. All my things remained in their usual place. On the liquor shelf the bottles stood, full or half drained, exactly as they had before. On the dresser everything was tidy and intact. On the table the tins of American coffee lay untouched.

I had been dreaming, I knew. A lovely, gentle, erotic dream. Then I looked again and saw scrawled across the dim, cracked surface of the wardrobe mirror a dark smear of lipstick: "I have taken some cigarettes for father," followed by several childish-looking kiss crosses.

I was glad of the kisses, but I didn't want Johnny to come in and see them. I don't know why—whether I was being protective to the girl or was feeling just plain possessive—either way I wanted to keep the mystery of her visit to myself. I knew exactly what Johnny would say. He'd laugh his loud riotous laugh and tell me I'd been had for a sucker. He would put his big paw on my shoulder and grin. "Never give a German girl an even break—even if she says she's Polish. Believe anything she says or does and she'll make a monkey out of you. It's the only way, Cap. Never take 'em seriously. The black market—now, you gotta take that real serious. That's money, that is, that's your future investment. But girls"—I

could imagine him shaking his tousled head, still grinning—
"never let 'em faze you."

With my flannel I quickly wiped out the message on the
mirror, expecting him to appear any minute.

All that remained of the dream were a few stubs in the
bedside ashtray and two sticky tumblers on the boards of the
uncarpeted floor.

Outside the open window a new, relief Polish sentry was
slowly sauntering past on his monotonous beat.

I looked at my watch: if I didn't hurry, the HQ cafeteria
would be closed. And I specially needed a good breakfast this
morning.

VIII

I liked Loot; he was a fine, healthy, whiskey-drinking, woman-loving, easy-going young American. And in my work with the American forces he was a key colleague of mine.

I use the word 'key' because he had charge of the motor transport and I needed a vehicle to take me on an urgent visit to British Army HQ. I had been asked by my colonel to make a personal report on the progress of my mission in Frankfurt. I thought if I took Loot along too the colonel would be less likely to kidnap, incarcerate, or otherwise detain me.

The major thought the visit a good idea and wanted me to convey an invitation to the colonel to make a return visit to us in Frankfurt. As for Loot I lured him into coming with tales of the legendary beauty of British servicewomen, and in particular with the reputed charm, vivacity, and redheadedness of a certain ATS whose name and whereabouts had been given to me by my cousin, whose friend she was, with some sort of injunction to 'look her up some time'.

We set out as merrily as a couple of sparrows, singing and whistling as the truck bounded along the autobahn. The dust flew, the sun shone; there was a haze on the hills, and the countryside quivered in the strong sun and vast blue sky. Every minute put our office and our work behind us another mile.

Loot started telling me about his wife, somewhere in the hills of Arkansas, and how much he missed her. And how be was looking forward to meeting a redhead; he had a real weakness for redheads, yessir. And he felt just ripe for a woman. Right now, yessir. Hell, he seemed to feel just ripe for a woman all the time in this goddam country. It seemed an awful long time to wait until we reached the British Zone. Couldn't we stop off in Kassel on the way and pick up a couple of German girls there? Uhh-uhh. He stretched at the wheel like a cat. There was no doubt he was fit.

The miles slid by as we tore along the concrete motorway, almost trafficless. The land rolled away on either side, flat and bare now, few hedges, no patchwork quilt of fields, just honest to God, hard-ploughed land, dragged over wearily by some tired out bullock or hoed laboriously by an old peasant woman, grim-looking and surly.

Along the verge from time to time we saw the tramps. They walked or stood or sat, alone, waiting for a lift. They were so far from anywhere that it seemed as though they didn't care where they were heading. They were on the move and that was all that mattered. They were tattered and grimed, and many of them crippled. There were so many one-legged men in Germany that one felt that the surgeons, grown desperate in the closing stages of the war, must have amputated any leg injury with a kind of weary automaticism.

"Serves the sons of bitches right," said Loot. "They're going no place. Most of them they're just on the run; they're no damn good. Look at all those women that come drifting in every night at the railroad station; they don't know where they're going or why they've come."

He had had some experience with them. He told me of one refugee who had come from a Polish concentration camp. She was just heading west. She looked about thirteen or fourteen at the most; but she was puny and kind of withered; and she had the dead expression of a zombie. All she knew was that she had to go westward.

"I picked her up, she seemed so childlike and helpless. She

looked scared, even when I gave her a chocolate bar she looked scared. Of course I couldn't sprechen Deutsch and she couldn't sprechen English so I took her round to my billet, so's she could have a square meal and freshen up a bit.

"Geez, I felt sorry for that kid. Say, how far is it from Poland? I wonder how she got that far. And she was so thin, just like a child before she grows up. So I took her into my room and do you know what was the first thing that goddam kid did? She went straight to my bed, set herself down, and lay there waiting.

"I guess she was the first chance of a bit of skirt I've turned down since I got posted to this goddam place. But some of these frauleins have just got to be seen to be believed. Tell me, what makes a guy go for all this stuff when he's got a swell wife waiting for him back home in Arkansas?"

I remembered the first night I spent in the American zone of Germany. That was before they sent me to the Polish compound. It was a late night temporary billet, with bare boards and straight-backed chairs and a hard steel bed. The window, which faced directly on to the bed, had no curtains. Nor did the window opposite of my neighbour, a US captain. The nights were warm and even at eleven darkness seemed hardly to have fallen. I could see the captain preparing himself for bed. Then there was the silhouette of a girl dressed in a black uniform; she undid her blouse, deftly slipped out of her skirt. When she took off her slip she was quite nude. The light in their room went out, and there was a sudden loneliness in mine.

I told Loot about this incident. He turned and gave me a big grin.

"Boy, what you need is a dame. You want to get you a fraulein."

He was right, of course, I did.

Then it happened. There we were travelling a good sixty, our thoughts full of sex, the hot sun pouring down and licking us with its big golden tongue. And on the grass 80 yards back from the road sat a siren, a black-haired Circe. She had a comb in her hand and was combing her loose shoulder-length hair. The sun lit her up.

"Wow," said Loot, and I caught my breath too. The brakes screeched. Loot's head had never turned back from the raven-haired roadside nymph. We must have stopped some three hundred yards on.

We looked at each other, with the same thought in mind. We were locked in a clash, like two rams when they are butting head to head.

"Wow," said Loot again and then he shook himself free and I could sense that he had suddenly remembered the redhead that I had in store for him in BAOR.

"Oh boy," he said. "Now's your chance. You take her behind that hedge. I'll give you ten minutes."

My legs wobbled like struck ninepins in a bowling alley. Nevertheless the beauty of the siren drew me on. There she was sitting still, combing. Her hair, blouse and skirt were black; arms, legs and face, white. As I came near, I fumbled for a packet of cigarettes, tearing open the container.

"Zigaretten?" I asked, and as I looked up I saw her fully for the first time.

The hair was black as matted coal, greasy. Her face was ageless—she could not have been twenty-five, yet it had a shrunk and cadaverous look, and as she smiled she showed several teeth missing; those that were left were yellow and black. Her thinness and flat chest made me suspect that she might be tubercular. TB, like typhus, was ravaging the country. Her legs, with her skirt pulled up high, were filthy and her clothes were stained with mud and grease. She took a cigarette and I could see her long, thin arms and her dirt-in-grained nails and hands.

I struggled to find something to say. "Wohin gehen Sie?" I asked at last.

She shrugged, with an indifference that was both abject and sly. She must have been dumped in the heart of the countryside by some truck driver unwilling to take her further. Where she went—or with whom—was immaterial; her destination was not a place, nor a person, it was simply survival.

"You like?" she said, indicating the hedge by a movement of her head, ingratiatingly.

All I wanted was an excuse to get away from her, quick. Loot was sitting there in the car, watching the seconds tick by on his watch. I was going to look an almighty fool, I thought with despair, returning to him to report mission unaccomplished.

"You like?" she repeated, her black eyes trying to calculate my reaction. As I looked into her eyes I could sense, behind their calculation, the pathos of one clutching at survival without hope.

"No, I don't like. We go talk." She looked puzzled. "Talk," I explained, pointing to the hedge. "Sprechen, verstehen?"

We went behind the hedge and when she finished smoking her cigarette, I shoved the rest of the packet into her hands and stumbled my way back to Loot.

"What's she like?" he inquired eagerly.

"Boy, you should have just seen her behind that hedge," I lied in reckless desperation. "I bet you never met anything like her."

He didn't wait for me to finish, but jumped out of the car in one almighty leap. I saw him fumble for his cigarette pack as he crashed through the hedge in real commando style. He was a very athletic man.

On his return he looked considerably shaken. We drove off and we didn't stop in Kassel after all, but pushed on to BAOR with grim determination. He told me that he was putting all his faith now in that redhead my cousin had wanted me to look up, and she'd better be good.

When we got to Herford the colonel decided he didn't want to see me after all, but left some message with a care-worn Adjutant about a shortage of officers. I passed on to the Adjutant the American major's invitation for the colonel to visit us. The Adjutant in return asked if I would do him a great favour. The Americans had in their PX stores a really wizard cure for hangovers. It was called Alka Seltzer. Could I possibly get him a couple of packets? Of course I would. He looked as though he needed them.

In the evening Loot and I went out with the Scots girl my cousin knew and a friend of hers. She turned out to be a nice and rather jolly lass, who taught him to say "It's a braw bricht moonlicht nicht the nicht." But that was as far as he got with her.

He was furious and wouldn't speak to me at all as we set off on the journey back.

I told him Colonel Furze was short of officers and he was lucky the colonel hadn't kept him as a hostage until the War Office sent a replacement.

That made him laugh. "OK," he said, "but I'll find my own dames in future."

IX

There was a distinctly cosmopolitan flavour about the headquarters of the United States Forces in Hoechst. Not only had
the Americans brought over with them typists, secretaries,
and clerical assistants of every allied nationality, blonde,
brunette and redhead; but there were several ex-enemy mis-
sions, as well as a group of Russians. The place where all
these nationalities were sure to meet was the immense
cafeteria that was the US officers' mess. And the one certain
time to meet them all was breakfast time. There between
half-past eight and nine you could be sure of finding almost
any foreign representative that you might wish to meet.

The Russians spoke to no one from the western countries.
They read the *New York Herald Tribune,* avidly from cover to
cover; but if anyone sat at their table and said, "Good morning," they did not understand; they looked at one another,
shook their heads, shrugged their shoulders, folded up their
papers, and took their leave. The Jugo-Slavs were very handsome, in smart grey uniforms; with them was a beautiful
blonde whose function clearly was to keep their interest from
straying to beautiful blondes who had been born in other
lands. The Hungarians brought with them Zara.

I saw her the first morning after her arrival in Frankfurt,
as I sat at the cafeteria table next to hers. Her Chief was lecturing her about the place, about her work, the people she
would work with, and the people she was to avoid. Zara was

not paying attention; her eyes wandered the length and breadth of the room. She had eyes that were pearl blue like those of a Siamese kitten. When they met mine there was an imperceptible smile. She said something to the old man—I suppose he was about sixty, quite heavy but not fat. With old-world gallantry he lifted himself out of his seat and made his way to the counter to fetch her the orange drink she requested. She smiled invitingly at me, as though it were a very funny thing that her Chief should get up and leave her, like a little boy at school doing the bidding of his teacher. I went over to her table and before the Chief returned, we'd arranged to go out to dinner that evening.

From that time on we were the closest friends. What gave Zara her special appeal was nothing physical, not her slim boyish figure, with short-cropped dark brown hair, nor her gleaming white teeth, nor her suntanned body that suited so well with her dark complexion. It was not even her courage or cool cheek; it was rather her devastating honesty. What she felt, what she thought, what she said, what she did—these were an integrated whole; there were no barriers of hesitation or hypocrisy. In defiance of convention she didn't care whether the conventions were bourgeois or communist.

I found her attractive in a wild and tomboyish way, but she merely laughed when I told her that she was beautiful.

"I am not beautiful. Wait until Judith comes, then you will see a beautiful woman."

"Judith?"

"They want another girl who won't go with a British officer or westerner. The Chief has threatened me so much that he realised that it is no good, so he asked for another girl. And they are sending my friend Judith."

"You know her?"

"We are old friends; in Budapest we lived together, and we shared many things. Judith has influence with a certain person who is placed very highly in the Government. First he got this job for me, now he arranges for Judith to come out of the country too. I told you she is very beautiful."

"And I tell you that you are."

"Just wait till you see her," she teased. "When you see Judith you will not think I am beautiful. She is more beautiful than me as I am than an old beggarwoman. Once you see Judith you will have no eyes for me."

Zara was right. Judith was more than beautiful, she was perfect. Her perfection was that of a classical painting: everything in her features, everything in her shape and colouring was in harmony.

It was at breakfast time in the cafeteria that I first saw her. There at one table sat the entire Hungarian mission; the Chief at the head, Zara as usual at one side of him, and Judith at the other. The remaining males sat in order of seniority on either side, the youngest, Ferenc, who loved Zara with unreturned passion, at the end. He glared at me, as he did every morning, ferociously. Nevertheless, whenever we passed each other he bowed to me. It was for Zara's sake that he committed these little icy gestures of politeness. Today, however, there was Judith; and Zara was grinning across the room, enjoying the sensation caused by her friend's presence.

Later in the morning she phoned my office.

"And what do you think of Judith? Was I not right? She is beautiful, don't you think?"

"Not just beautiful, perfect."

Zara's laugh tinkled down the telephone.

"Not perfect, I think, but very beautiful, as I told you."

I heard a giggle in the background and knew that Judith was close beside her friend.

"She has asked if she might meet you."

"Tonight," I said, "for dinner. At the Castle Kronberg."

As we ate in the candlelit room of the ancient castle, the soft light flickered on her black hair and dark eyes and smooth satiny skin. The red rose which she wore at the V of her black dress against the white of her skin seemed to be not just a decoration, but a part of her. Something of its fragrance and smoothness became an extension of her own beauty. It seemed incredible that I should be sitting there with someone so beautiful.

After dinner, we wandered through the vast rooms of the castle with their heavy paintings, in gilt frames, of former royal owners staring indifferently over us. Judith only drew me closer to her. Outside, in the garden, she turned towards me and slipped expertly into my arms for me to kiss her.

And so the curious but inevitable affair with Judith now began. To me she was like a living masterpiece of painting or of sculpture. What I liked best in our most intimate meetings was to look at the whiteness of her body, to feel the softness and smoothness of her skin; to watch her movements, supple and graceful, as she dressed or moved about the room. After all these years, I have no other memories of her. I cannot think of a single sentence she said to me or that I spoke to her. Zara gave warmth and life; Judith glittered like a diamond in a cool, hard light.

I began to see Judith one evening and Zara the next. Neither girl made reference to this arrangement, and so when the day's work was over, I floated through the long summer evenings, all tensions set aside; the Americans forgotten, the Germans sealed away as if they were non-existent. With these two Hungarian girls, ex-enemies, now collaborators, I felt at ease and secure. And yet as the weeks went by I experienced a mild surprise that neither seemed to resent the other's relationship with me.

"Have you been yet to Heidelberg?" Zara asked one day. To me Heidelberg was a place of romance and history, and she knew that I wanted to visit it.

"Let's spend the day together there next week," she urged. "The Commission has some business there; if I speak to the

Chief he will let me go to see to it in the car; and I can take you with me. "

Zara was as good as her word. Early on the appointed morning the Hungarians' large old limousine appeared outside my billet. Zara was sitting beside the driver in the front seat. In the back of the car, tucked under a large motoring rug, was Judith.

"Zara didn't say that you were coming too," I said. "I'm flattered."

Judith smiled.

"The Chief didn't like the idea of Zara going on such a long journey alone. Perhaps he suspected that she might want to take you with her."

Judith was in a very teasing mood throughout the journey. She flirted with me openly; she snuggled up to me underneath her rug. Her hands wandered clingingly over my body, so that I was compelled to wrap the rug around myself also; but that brought us even closer and gave Judith more opportunity still. Zara didn't seem to mind in the least, however closely Judith clung; she merely turned and smiled at us.

Disembarking from the car in Heidelberg, Zara linked arms with Judith and Judith linked arms with me and both girls were happy and carefree as we set out to explore the town. We visited the castle and wine cellars; we looked down on the river and the town from the height; we walked the 'philosopher's way'. Gay, romantic, full of sunshine, the town matched our mood. Heidelberg had been one of the few towns undamaged by bombs and so we were able to forget the war and all its consequences.

When evening came we made our way back to the car. The chauffeur stood waiting, shifting his weight from one huge foot to another, looking down at his blackened boots, his expression concealed. Zara spoke to him sharply in Hungarian.

"The man is a fool," she turned to explain, "there is some trouble with the car, which he can't put right."

He was an idiot, she assured us, a peasant who had learned to drive in the army, and who was more at home with a plough than a car.

"What's wrong with it?"

"He must get it to a garage for repairs, and we will journey home tomorrow. Now we go and have a drink. We can decide about a hotel later. After all," she added, "it isn't often that we are together all three. Often two together, but rarely three."

As we sat drinking, the girls seemed quietly happy, glancing at each other and smiling in that understanding way that women have when they share a secret denied to their male companion. When I suggested we looked for a lodging, Zara smiled at Judith. "We shall find somewhere later; why spoil a good evening?"

Judith smiled back. "Leave it to Zara; there are always lodging houses if you know where to go."

We argued about this over our drinks on and off most of the evening. Judith, though she said little herself, backed up Zara, even while her leg was stroking mine beneath the table. Indeed, the more she agreed with everything Zara said, the more she seemed intent upon manifesting her intimacy with me. She hugged my arm when we walked, she squeezed herself close as we sat, she snuggled up tightly as she had done in the car; her hand sought mine constantly so that I had to keep my elbows on the table, and then her leg would glide underneath the table in a secondary surreptitious search. But Zara in her bright-eyed reckless fashion seemed to see nothing of this; she went on quaffing her beer with vigour and gusto. Nothing that Judith did seemed to cast a shadow of suspicion into the mind of Zara.

At last the bars began to close and we set out in search of somewhere to lodge. Zara guided us confidently through the narrow streets, and soon picked out a house.

The door was opened by a German woman, big-boned, elderly, severe. As Zara began arguing with her about our requirements, Judith slipped her body against mine and was nuzzling me softly, trying to make me take her in my arms, while Zara in harsh guttural German was intent on battering down the reluctance of the woman at the door. Zara's argument drove home. The woman shrugged her shoulders and nodded in the direction of the interior. We climbed the twisting, creaking stairs and entered an old-fashioned room. It had a high ceiling, a table, several straight-backed chairs, a broken-down old armchair, and one large double bed.

"This will do, yes?" Zara enquired of Judith. Their eyes turned to the large double bed with a satisfied, appreciative look. Judith inspected the bed, pursing her beautiful lips as though in doubt, as she lowered herself on to its edge. She stretched herself backwards into its soft centre, and let her legs dangle over the side.

"It will do," she murmured.

"Where's my room?" I asked.

Judith gave me an enigmatic little smile. Zara shrugged.

"This is all she had. At first she was not willing to let us have this. She said that she would get into trouble to let her room to American troops. I had to bribe her very heavily. It was difficult to make her understand that we were not Americans. So I told her we were all three Hungarians."

Uneasily I was aware of being trapped and somehow at their mercy.

"I also said that you were my brother."

Zara paused while the two of them enjoyed the joke.

"Why are you so cross? Perhaps it is because you do not want to spend the night with us both? Perhaps you want to spend the night with Judith, yes?"

"Or with Zara I think," giggled Judith.

The landlady brought in our supper: a bottle of rough red wine and some hunks of bread and cheese on a tray. The girls were in high spirits, treating this meal as though it were a royal feast. They cut the cheese into three portions, carved the bread into three thick slices, and poured equal amounts of wine into the three tumblers. It was a game that they were playing, that everything had to be equally shared: the wine, the food, and later, they insisted, the bed also.

The food stood on the plates in chunky portions, and the wine settled thickly in its three crude glasses.

"Come and eat," urged Zara.

But I didn't like the prospect of being reduced to the same status as a bottle of rough red wine and a hunk of German cheese.

Zara grinned.

"You may as well, how you say?—make the best of a bad job. After all, a lot of men would be only too glad to find themselves in this position."

After supper they prepared for bed and began to undress unconcernedly. They lay quietly in the large double bed, each with one arm round the other's shoulder. Their soft, smooth faces looked relaxed and deceptively innocent, but beneath their demure eyelids I could sense their eyes trembling with mirth, and I knew then that their friendship was unbreakable.

I switched out the light and curled up uncomfortably on the worn-out old armchair. For a while I heard Judith's giggles; then, as the two girls turned towards each other in a final embrace, the sounds subsided into a relaxed and peaceful slumber.

For some time after that experience I took pains to avoid dating either of them. I was a bit huffed, wanted to show I could manage without them, I suppose. I pretended not to see them at mealtimes as they sat happily together with the other Hungarians at their table in the huge cafeteria mess.

Moreover, I was very busy back at the I&E office during the day; and in the evenings I had to spend some time entertaining a British author whom the Tourist Board had sent over to talk to the troops about ancient buildings. In fact Edmund Vale was both an enthusiast and an expert and I knew he would make his subject interesting enough not to create any boredom riots among the troops.

"It's all so different from the army in my day," he said. "But still, so's everything else."

There were two places he particularly wanted to visit. One was Heidelberg, the other was Hamelin. I couldn't get him a fixture at Heidelberg (and I didn't tell him about my own visit), but I managed to send him off to Pied Piper land. He was a charming man, whose goodbye gift of an autographed book on old churches I still treasure.

Such civilised company had cheered me up, so that when he had gone I rang Zara. I told her I had seen the funny side of our night in Heidelberg. She was pleased. "You British are so easily shocked," she said. "But I prefer that to what the Russians did when they came to Budapest."

"And Judith?" I asked cautiously.

"Oh that's all right," said Zara. "That's been taken care of." It seemed that in the meantime Judith had turned her attentions to a very blond and handsome Norwegian. The Chief had been furious, and Zara said that he was going to send her home and ask for another Hungarian girl instead.

She would be beautiful, of course; but however beautiful she might be, there would be no more trips to Heidelberg.

X

In spite of everything, I had a personal liking for those who worked in our I&E section—the major because of his eternal optimism, Loot because like me, he was just seeing the whole crazy business through until demob, Julie because we now had a sort of secret understanding, and I even felt sorry for her companion typist, Madame, the old lady from the Resistance. All the same I missed my old messmates of BAOR and of earlier days on Salisbury Plain.

I remembered almost with affection how day after day I had signed interminable forms to requisition or to receive upon delivery bewildering quantities of books or educational equipment. For these were things I understood. And behind me to stop me making a fool of myself there was always Sergeant May, centre half and goalkeeper, stock bowler and long stop extraordinaire.

Here, I never knew what role might suddenly be thrust upon me. The major believed in putting into practice every new idea that burgeoned in his head. Nor did he mind failure, since for each idea that died the death he would have unlimited new ideas to replace it.

By pestering relentlessly, he'd got the French to promise to send a team to the inter-allied goodwill section. He was a bit surprised, but none the less elated, to learn that they were to be two young women from the Department of Defence.

"A coupla ooh-la-las from Paris to represent France, eh?"

crowed Loot. "That's a master-stroke, they'll really take the troops by the balls." He grinned at me in a special sort of way, as if to remind me of his own unfortunate experience with the Scots girl in BAOR.

A desk or two away I heard Julie sniff contemptuously, whereupon Madame stood up ramrodlike and with a signal to Julie led their protest march to the loo.

"Competition," said Loot. "Wow, I can look forward to that."

"Shucks," groaned the major, "that's another half hour's typing gone." But his restless mind was already moving to a new idea. "Say, why don't you get some nice British girl to come over and do some typing?"

He didn't wait for a reply but grabbed the phone. Another new and more important idea had struck him.

"American Forces Network—AFN," he said. "Say, I wanna tell you about these two French dames who're coming to I&E." He listened to something at the other end of the line. "Yeah, to I&E, part of our inter-allied goodwill programme. You could make a good story outa this." And on he went, cooking up a most splendid yarn about how these girls had been specially selected for their appeal to US troops. Vive la France, huh?—vive Lafayette and don't forget Vive Major Haynes of I&E.

I took a little Union Jack out of a drawer in my desk and placed it in a sort of tubular pot designed for pencils. It drooped rather self-consciously.

"Hey," said Loot, "I can see you're going to have quite a time worrying how to cope with that ooh-la-la competition."

Knowing the British military machine would regard with incomprehension any suggestions I might make as to how best they might compete with a couple of Frenchwomen in winning the goodwill of the US troops, I struggled to think of means by which my reports might by-pass my colonel in BAOR. By now I was convinced that my reports sent to the War Office were not getting through. I was out on my own;

and there seemed nothing I could do about it.

On the Monday when the Frenchwomen arrived, we were all agog to see them, but the major didn't bring them into the office right away. We saw him take them along the corridor to his own colonel, who was in another part of the building. (I suspect the colonel had placed the inter-allied section so far away because he didn't want to be too closely identified with this oddball outfit and all its potential for dangerous political consequences). After introduction to the colonel, the major brought them round to the office. They looked smart in their dark blue uniform, very chic; and very businesslike in their expressions. As I told Loot later I couldn't see much ooh-la-la there.

"Uh-uh," he agreed. "They look sour. Reckon I'd rather make a pass at Julie—and that's saying sump'n."

"Julie's not so bad," I said, but casually so he wouldn't suspect I'd been up to anything.

"Well, mebbe. What she needs is to sweat a couple of stone off. I could think of a coupla ways—"

"Those two Frenchwomen," I interrupted, knowing where his thoughts invariably tended, "looked too damn serious."

"A dead loss, I guess," Loot said, and turned to the paper work on his desk.

The major, however, was so excited on the day of their arrival that he couldn't stop talking at them, going on about the wonderful things our section was doing right now and about his big plans for the future. They stared at him.

Thinking that more was needed he waved his hand expressively in my direction. "Our representative from the UK," he said.

The two Frenchwomen swivelled their stare in my direction. "Where's the Russian?" they asked, unimpressed. Their English was excellent.

Before the major could get around to explaining the political difficulties, Loot cut in. "He's in Moscow," he grinned.

"We're in negotiation," said the major. "but they're sure to send someone now we've got the French."

The girls gave a little smirk. "It's not that simple," the senior of them said sharply. "I think we'll go back to the hotel now to prepare for our talk on radio AFN you are arranging for us."

"Sure," said the major. "Loot here will find you some transport. Now, and any time you need it."

"Of course," said the one.

"Naturally," said the other.

"You bet," said Loot.

"Well, what d'ya think?" said the major when they had left.

My thought ran along the lines that maybe if I wore a skirt I'd get proper transport too. Instead I said "Those aren't *army* uniforms, you know."

The major squirmed a little. "The girls are from the Ministry of Defence. They've got officer status."

"Why *two* of them? Isn't there an officer shortage in France?"

"That's right," agreed the major. "That's why they've sent two *women*. We're in luck, having two, that's a 40 per cent increase in our section staff. Say, couldn't you ask your War Office to send you another guy too? Or ATS," he added hurriedly, catching my withering look.

"What's this about their giving a talk on AFN?"

"That's something they're dead nuts on," said the major. "I was able to fix it for them with the colonel."

"Time we had a talk on Britain too."

"Sure," said the major uncertainly, "sure."

"Well, then, will you fix it for me with your colonel?"

"Look," said the major. "In confidence," and he began to stride around the room in troubled restlessness. "It's like this. These two French dames want to use modern technology and entertainment expertise. Not all this old-fashioned travelling up and down the country to little groups, but radio chat shows that will get across to millions. That's an idea that's OK with us. It'll get our section on the air. It's modern, it's effective, and it'll bring the work of our section to everyone's attention."

"Then get me on too."

"Aw, hell," said the major, stopping at his desk and cracking one solitary knuckle. "You don't know what you're asking. AFN will give us only one slot, and that's for these French dames. Jeez, if I had my way I'd have the French today, the Brits tomorrow, the Russkis the day after. I'd like that, I sure would, but we gotta be realists, Cap, and all I got is one slot."

"Which is for the French?"

"Sure. This is the deal we made with them."

"I've a better deal," I said. "We double the programme's length, make it a BIG one, and we *all* go on the air—you, me, and the French girls. It'll be a live debate—no holds barred— you know, like which country's done more in the cause of allied goodwill, which country has the prettiest girls, which country can offer the best holiday, which country you'd most like to live in and why?"

"Hey, hold on," said the major, "you've got something there. Yessir. I guess we've got to go for the big one." He reached for the telephone.

"Lemme talk to Chuck. Yeah, Chuck. Hi ya, Chuck, I've just got some great news for you. You know that slot for the two French dames, well we've come up with a great new idea. Do you wanna know? Well, right ..." He went on at speed for about five minutes. It began to sound hopeful. He put the phone down at last. "It's on," he gasped.

We didn't see the girls the next day, nor the major. I guessed he was squaring the circle with them and his colonel and AFN and anybody else who needed fixing for the new deal to come off.

On Wednesday morning he was already in the office when I arrived.

"The debate's to be on Friday night. 20.00 hours. Prime time. You, me, and the mamselles. Live."

"Great."

"Yeah, I've arranged for us all to meet at 11.00 hours this morning in Frankfurt to discuss arrangements and what sort of line we're going to take on the issues which arise."

"Did you say in Frankfurt?"

"Yeah, we're meeting the mamselles at their hotel."

"That reminds me," I said. "How come they're staying in a top-class hotel? I'm in a billet with Poles and blackmarketers, you're in the US compound with your wife. What makes them so special?"

"Aw, it's just diplomacy. We'd put everybody in a first class hotel if we could. A couple of women ... we can't set 'em down *any*where. You have to work different ways with different people."

"They haven't been into the office to work yet," I pointed out. "So what's going on?"

"It's nothing. Just a little hitch with their Ministry of Defence, something bureaucratic. A bit like your guys, huh?"

We had our planning session in a discreet corner of the hotel lounge. The two French ladies looked very determined. The senior was called Françoise, the younger Delphine. They sat, in their chic but office-like uniforms, bottoms clenched on the edge of their chairs, as if to indicate that serious business was about to begin.

I sat opposite them, lounging as carelessly as I could, and the major took the chair between us.

"We've only got forty minutes on the air, so we want to make good use of it," he began. This AFN guy, Chuck, will give us a lead-in. First of all we ought to give a short history or account of how the inter-allied goodwill scheme originated in the US Army, then—"

"Who's going to do that?" interrupted Françoise.

The major blinked. "I am," he said. "As head of the section which conceived the scheme, I reckon I'm the most suitable person to give the introduction."

"OK," said Françoise. "I just wanted to get everything clear. A short introduction, ha? Very short, I should hope, so it is not too boring."

"Actually," I put in, "the origin of the scheme could be a very interesting story. I heard it in London. There was this young NCO—straight out of Harvard who had the vision to see that those who had been allied in war needed something extra to hold them together during the occupation—and in the peace that would follow."

The major was fidgeting in his chair. "That may be," he interrupted, "but it was before my posting to the section, so I don't think we can go all that far back into names and credits and all that stuff."

Françoise looked at Delphine. Then she said, "Go on, captain. Tell us what they told you in London."

"Well, I heard the story at our War Office, where they were quite impressed by the nerve of this young American corporal. He'd put his scheme up to the GOC US forces in Germany and they'd shelved it, thinking they wouldn't get any of the other three powers interested. So the corporal took his next leave in London and sat on the doorstep of Sir Ronald Adam—he was the adjutant general of the British Army at that time. Sir Ronald knew that Americans are a democratic people and that rank didn't cut much ice with them and that, anyway, all good ideas got blocked trying to find their way through official channels—I mean, that's what official channels are for, aren't they? Sir Ronald was intrigued to find a Harvard graduate corporal sitting on his doorstep. He took him to dinner at his club and over the coffee and liqueur said, 'What a marvellous idea. You're on.' And that's how it all began."

The major seemed momentarily speechless.

101

"Do you mean," Françoise interposed in her severest voice "that this inter-allied project was—how do you say?—cooked up between the British and the Americans? Did this anonymous young corporal go to Paris to invite the French?"

"The legend as I heard it," I said "recounts no such visit."

"You mean," said Delphine, as though not believing her ears, "the French were not a full and equal part of this arrangement?"

"It's just so much water under the bridge," urged the major. "I never heard anything of this story. It was all before my time."

"Well," said Françoise rising, and Delphine with her, "we cannot accept this. I shall have to report back to Paris."

"Listen," called the major, jumping up, "we can scrap the historical background introduction, and I'll just say a few words about how things stand now."

But the girls were already marching out. "We go to phone the Ministry," Françoise shot the words over her shoulder.

"Oh hell," groaned the major, sinking back into his chair and looking sorrowfully at me, "You've ballsed it all up—there goes my medal."

I didn't know what he meant by his medal, until months later. One day he said to me when I was preparing my report to BAOR, "Do you think you could suggest to your people that it would help the work of our section if they could hand out some sort of medal? In recognition, you know, of my function here."

I looked at him in amazement. I had a naive idea that medals were for valour. "Oh," he said, suddenly realising something was amiss. "I'd do the same for you, with our people."

Next day the major told me the broadcast was on after all. The Ministry in Paris had told the girls to take part. The office was in quite a buzz about it. Julie, head down, fingers plonking on the typewriter keys, had been looking at me out of the corner of her eyes. At midday when nobody else was in the office, Madame went to the loo and Julie did not accompany her, pretending she had so much work to finish.

"You must be careful," she whispered, "at tomorrow's broadcast. You know, those two Frenchwomen are trained for this. That is their job in Paris for the Ministry. That is why they will not go on tours like you and your British speakers. They want only to use the radio. They are very skilled and there are two of them, they will eat you alive." She looked at me with expressionless face and her deep mournful eyes. "Be careful," she said.

I gave her a little thank you butterfly kiss on the black hair over her forehead. "It's all right," I bragged. "I've done my research."

Julie was right: the broadcast was a death trap. We sat around the studio table with a giant microphone in front of us and waited for the green light to come on. The major got off to a good start, then Françoise and Delphine chattered away, one sparking the other, cutting in on each other and both interrupting the major or me whenever we tried to take the air. I held on tight to my notes about things in which the UK excelled and waited eagerly for a chance to bring them in. There seemed no point, however, at which I could break into the conversation, so fluently it moved. It went on and on, rapid fire. The major fought manfully to make a few interjections and seemed satisfied as long as he could plug in key words like USA, I&E, Major Haynes. I had a desperate feeling that I was letting the side down, for this was not a polite BBC sort of conversation but a cut-throat scramble for airtime. I tried to speed up my reactions but the French girls left me no opening. Françoise and Delphine were dishing out facts over the air about French technology; they'd already done the stuff about French women, French food, French education, French holiday resorts until you could believe France was Paradise, Utopia, and the Garden of Eden all rolled into one. Now they were into France's wonderful skills in engineering, construction, airplanes, railway trains—you name it, the French were the world's best.

"We move with the times," Françoise proclaimed. "We are not stuck in the past like some countries."

"Like Britain for example," fed in Delphine.

"We are a quick, alive people," Françoise went on, "quick in our emotions, quick in thought and speech, alert to new ideas."

The studio light turned to a warning amber, showing that our time was almost up. I made a last desperate effort. "I'd like to say something too," I burst out with such sudden force that every one stopped and looked at me. "You've got the wrong idea about the British. You think we're slow in speech and slow to react, you think we're conservative and technologically backward and nothing's ever changed with us. So, let me enlighten you. Who's the fastest man in the world? On water Sir Malcolm Campbell, speed 142 m.p.h. British. On land John Cobb, speed 370 m.p.h. British. In the air—if you listen to Françoise and Delphine I suppose you'll think it's a Frenchman and I guess Major Haynes would say it's bound to be an American. But I can tell you, it's another Limey: Group Commander Wilson flying a British meteor jet, speed 508 m.p.h. We're the fastest people on earth, when we want to be, and we've the best technology. On land, on water, in the air—it's in the record books."

The major looked astounded, the French girls looked furious. To hell, I thought, with inter-allied goodwill. Suddenly we were off the air. Then the major began to laugh, as though it had all been a great success. The producer came bursting in.

"That was great," he enthused. "That punch line of yours was just a wow. I can see the protest mail coming in right now. It was real inspiration to save it up till the end like that."

"Save it up be hanged," I protested. "I'd have blurted it out in the first five minutes, if they'd only have let me get a word in."

Next week in the office neither the major nor the French liaison team came in. Julie and Madame were busy sorting out the major's mail and papers. I could see them chattering with unusual animation, eyes sparkling, heads wagging. "Perhaps," I heard Julie whisper, "we could tell the captain?"

The old lady looked at me, almost benignly I thought. "Ja," she nodded, "Why not?" They both giggled.

"Later," said Julie as she saw me looking and bent her black head down towards her typewriter. Madame whispered something to her and then made her usual exit.

Julie looked up and smiled at me. "I have good news to tell you," she said. "The Frenchwomen—Madame and I do not like them. We do not want them in the office, they are so very cold. So we are very happy to learn," she shook a little note which had lain on her desk, "that they have gone back to Paris."

"I don't think they liked our section," I hazarded.

"No," said Julie "they never intended to stay. Just to come and do one big broadcast. The major is very disappointed."

I looked into her deep brown eyes and remembered our evening together. "Julie, I seem to recall I owe you a dinner. Why don't we go out tonight and celebrate?"

She smiled.

"This time, I would like very much to get to the Castle."

"OK," I agreed.

"I suppose," she added, "you wouldn't take Madame too?"

XI

The US army transport office in Hoechst was situated in a large vehicle yard just off the main street. It had once been part of the I.G. Farben chemical plant and the huge grey walls of that building frowned down on the street untouched, amazingly, by the bombs of war. Common opinion was that the allies had spared I.G. Farben deliberately, because they wanted to take it over for themselves after the war, a view which ascribed a remarkable accuracy to the US army air force.

True enough, the offices were now used by the American I&E for their administrative centre and the goods yard for their own transport vehicles.

There, outside the transport office, stood a single waiting jeep. I reached it from one side just as Angel reached it from the other. Like me, she was holding a little white chit which officially authorised one to use the jeep. The German driver looked at us with helpless perplexity: chivalry inclined him to the woman, soldierliness to the officer. We both waved our chits vigorously. Angel bit her lip and stamped her foot. Neither of us was willing to give way. The tension was such that it took a few angry glares before we discovered that we were both heading for the same HQ office in Frankfurt and therefore might as well travel together.

Angel was well named. Her face was soft and innocent-looking; she had that traditional English roses-and-rainwater complexion. She wore a light, silk dress which fluttered gracefully when she moved. She seemed as if she had stepped straight from the English country house scene.

It must have been the sunlight streaming from that halo of golden hair, and her air of being part of an England that I was missing that attracted me to her. I didn't intend this to happen because I had a more or less regular companionship now with Zara.

For Angel our relationship was equally an involuntary slip. For she was engaged to an American colonel and her plans were quite firmly that he should take her back with him to the States to be wed. Indeed, he was an excellent catch; an American of good family background, well-off, Princeton and West Point, reasonably handsome, only a few years older than Angel, a regular soldier well on his way up. Moreover, Dick worshipped Angel, with her English upper class air, in that rather idealising way about women that some Americans have.

Angel made it clear that she didn't want our relationship to ruin her engagement to Dick, her steady bread and butter attachment as one might say. Although I was happy to co-operate, the problem was that Angel lost her head whenever Zara appeared.

Angel's complicated efforts to conceal our relationship from Colonel Dick gave Zara a great deal of scornful amusement. There was one unquestionable advantage, however, which Angel had: Angel was allied personnel, whereas Zara was ex-enemy alien. This gave Angel entry to many places which were forbidden to Zara. The officers' midsummer dance for instance. It is probable that one of the chief reasons why Angel invited me to this dance was that she thought she would demonstrably score over Zara. The more so because on this particular occasion her colonel was acting as host, with Angel as hostess.

True enough, Zara was rather nettled when I told her of

Angel's invitation.

"Angel is a big cream bun—she is a cream puff. I am surprised she does not make you sick," she said. Then she said, "She likes to stand, all sugary, like a cake on a pedestal while you admire her. Wait till you see inside the icing."

"Very dishy icing," I said. Still, I thought about that pedestal bit; Angel did rather like one to look up to her as if she was some precious icon.

Zara grinned and said, "We have an old Hungarian saying that he who rides two horses successfully must be a circus acrobat. Angel likes too much her pedestal to be an acrobat."

"Jealousy will get you nowhere: old English saying."

"I suppose you think that I spend another dull evening with Ferenc, while you dance with Angel. Pooh!—we shall see."

On the night of the dance the canteen was all lit up, with little coloured lanterns; and a German civilian orchestra, trying hard to look merry and bright, feverishly scraped out the favourite American tunes of the day. Soon the party seemed to be going with a swing. Angel came to sit with me every now and then while Dick was at the bar. She was in a very happy mood, grateful for my understanding about Dick, flushed with the success of her organising efforts, and delighted at her skill in having both her men safely in tow. What with the music, the champagne, the little lantern lights, the glow of happiness—Angel was on top of the world. I watched her perform on the dance floor with Dick; she was in great form. Thoroughly alive and yet untouchably cool and elegant. Then suddenly her body stiffened as though she had been shot; her steps halted; her gaze was transfixed.

At the entrance to the hall stood Zara, clothed in a white evening dress, her short-cropped hair gleaming wickedly black. She wore long white gloves beyond which her bare arms rose a golden demerara to her shoulders. An impudent smile stretched across her suntanned face. By her side was Ferenc, flashily handsome in his grey-green uniform. He was her regular standby. She didn't encourage his infatuation, but she found him useful whenever she needed an escort.

When she caught sight of me, she spoke to Ferenc sharply. He saluted and left. Zara moved towards my table, smiling; her teeth were very white and very even.

Seeing Zara arrive, Angel, who was in the middle of the dance floor, broke from her partner, pushed her way through the dancers, and met her face to face. Their eyes flashed like points of steel. I could see the lace frills of Angel's dress front rise and fall before she trusted herself to speak.

"Enemy aliens are not permitted in here."

"Ex-enemy."

"That," said Angel icily, "is purely a quibble."

"I think I like it here," murmured Zara, looking with interest at the paper lanterns swinging in the heated air. "The decorations are nice."

Angel turned to her colonel. "Dick, tell her she's not permitted in."

"Oh, but I am." Zara smiled and looked at me. "I am here as the captain's guest."

I took a deep breath. "Of course," I lied.

Angel turned furiously on her heel. "Take me to the bar, Dick. I don't want to be in the same room as that enemy alien bitch."

Zara found Angel's discomfiture highly entertaining. She settled down at my table and we sat there drinking and talking, listening to the music and watching the dancers—it was impossible not to have fun with Zara. Soon we had finished our bottle of champagne, and it was time to get another.

As I pushed my way through the crowd that gathered around the bar, I saw Angel, flushed and angry, drinking there with Dick. By the way she was tipping down her cognac, it was clear that she was in a reckless mood. When she saw me I heard her ask Dick to fetch some cigarettes. The moment he was gone she grabbed me by the arm.

"Darling, don't let that little Hungarian come between us. Promise me one thing. Please, after what you've done to me tonight, promise me just one thing."

"Look, Angel, you know I didn't invite Zara here—"

"Promise me you'll not go back with her. Promise me you'll come home with me tonight."

She was more sloshed than I had thought.

"OK," I said. I didn't want her to spoil her evening by getting stupidly drunk.

Then she suddenly remembered. "But I have to stay behind to help Dick clear up. Please, darling, just promise that you will go straight to my apartment. Here's my spare key, let yourself in. Don't wait for me if I'm late, just go to bed. I shall come home just as quickly as I can."

The dance continued its confused gaiety, and after a time even Angel came back on to the floor. But when she and Dick passed the swinging lanterns near our table, she seemed to become aware of Zara's grinning. She began to make mistakes in her steps and finally left the floor for good, heading for the bar with the devoted Dick following dejectedly behind her.

Then, in no time at all, it seemed, the clock was striking one, the band was playing the final dance, the bar closed, the lanterns went out over the tables. Somewhere backstage, Angel and Dick were beginning rather drunkenly to organise the clearing away.

"Ferenc will be waiting with the car," Zara said. "Let us drop you on your way."

It was Ferenc's mission to see Zara safely home, rescued from the bourgeois gaiety. As he dropped me off at the spot I indicated, he gave his little icy good night bow, and Zara waved her white gloved hand.

I thought I ought to make it up to Angel by keeping my promise to wait for her at her flat. So, entering with the key she had given me, I switched on the light, sat down, and drank a whiskey. I flicked through the pages of the latest issue of the *Stars and Stripes,* the US forces' newspaper. Bored, I turned to an old copy of *Country Life* which Angel kept to remind herself of home and also, I suspected, to impress Dick with her gentrified background. They were certainly taking their time clearing the premises and saying goodnight. It seemed a good idea to turn off the light and go to bed.

What woke me was a light shining through the frosted window of the bedroom door and the noise of voices, a male American voice which sounded as though it was making suggestions and a female English voice, making no resistance. As I sat up in bed, alerted to danger, the voices came nearer and I could hear Angel asking Dick if he would like a drink first and Dick saying hadn't they had enough to drink already?

"Frailty, thy name is woman," I thought and I was still sitting bolt upright in nude but stately dignity, when the door opened.

Angel stood with her hand on the door handle, and we stared at each other for a second in amazement, like two statues from a forgotten past. It took Angel just that tiny fraction of time to sober up. All those patient months she had put in playing the grand English lady, proving to her up-and-coming young colonel how dignified she was and how marriage-worthy, were now at stake.

With her hand still on the door handle, she swung round, her bosom thrust out like a shield. "Dick, this is my *bedroom* … You can't come in here."

In the same movement she had snapped the door shut. There was a sound of scuffling and I could hear Dick splutter, "What the hell—?"

"No, Dick. I absolutely forbid it. You may not enter my bedroom."

There was more spluttering by Dick, but she had got him away from the door. They seemed to be talking in low, angry voices. Then I heard Angel say, "Dick, I think you ought to go home now. I never thought you would behave like this. Dick, I will give you one more drink and I expect you to leave like a gentleman."

I don't think he wanted his drink, for a moment later I heard the front door slam with quite ungentlemanly violence.

Angel came into the bedroom. "Blast you," she said resentfully, kicking off one evening shoe so that it struck the bedside wall, "and blast," she added, kicking off the other, "that enemy alien bitch."

As she came over to the bed there were tears in her eyes. "How could you," she reproached, "how could you do this to me?" Her lips pouted as they trembled and her wonderful halo of hair was shining by the bedlamp pure gold. She looked like a figure in a Burne-Jones stained glass window. A martyred virgin perhaps.

"Come to bed," I teased "and think of England."

"Stuff England," she wailed angrily, "I want my Dick."

We remained friends, but she never really forgave me for Zara's appearance at the dance, even though she was able to patch things up with Dick.

I hadn't much to say for myself really. Things had started out as fun; but as time and my months of service ground on they began to seem pointless or desperate or increasingly absurd. I wish this bloody occupation was over, I kept thinking.

XII

When the major did a thing he did not do it by halves. He was proud of the fact that he was a natural 'promoter'. I shall always remember the dinner party he gave to celebrate his wife's arrival from the US. He had been writing to her every day for months, long intimate manuscript letters. I used to see him poring over them at his office desk, with his sharp, angular nose pointing so far down at the paper that one almost expected him to dip it into the ink from time to time; blinking furiously through his thick spectacles as he wrote. He never looked up, never needed to stop for thought. He seemed to have only one object, to persuade his wife to leave their Philadelphia home, come to Germany and settle down in the American forces' married quarters in Frankfurt. There was something quaint, a little old-fashioned and rather romantic in his attachment.

We never really expected his wife to materialise. When she did, it was a great surprise and for a week or two we hardly saw the major, as he set up home.

"I'd sure like you to come to dinner to meet the wife," he beamed one day. "We're having a little party, so come along and, say, it would be an idea to bring a girl friend with you."

I would like to have brought Zara, but obviously I couldn't bring an ex-enemy alien to this particular do. I gathered from the invitations that were streaming out from the office that the affair was mushrooming into something large and rather formal. So to impress the major I decided to invite Angel to accompany me.

She seemed an ideal partner in this game of upholding British prestige amid the all-surrounding Americans. Her conventional upper middle-class background gave her a kind of haughty unapproachability so that, when she relaxed and smiled, it seemed an act of incomparable graciousness. It was this ambivalence which both confused and challenged, that made some men go quite silly about her. In short, she gave an outward air of cool distinction which no other female I knew in Frankfurt could equal.

When we arrived at the hotel at which the party was being held, the gathering was much larger and more formal than I had expected. The major had cast his net wide, including in his invitation representatives from every nation that happened to have any of its nationals in Frankfurt in any kind of capacity whatever. It was as though a session of the United Nations had transformed itself into the major's dinner party. There he was, beaming at us through his spectacles and looking benign. His wife was at his side, and no wonder he had spent his days and nights writing her long letters; for she was a striking woman, some years younger than himself, who stood out even among the other attractive women present.

For the major this was his great day of triumph. Placing his guests at a series of adjoining tables arranged diplomatically in a large circle, he sat surrounded by representatives of nearly all the European allied countries, and some neutral states as well, and I could see that high-ranking US officers also present were just as surprised as I was at the extent of the major's little party which seemed to cast him as the military ambassador in chief to all foreign nationalities in the American Zone of Germany.

As we sipped our wine we became quickly immersed in holding our own in this curiously cosmopolitan gathering. Angel, seated on my right, found herself next to a civilian gentleman from the Ministry of Foreign Affairs in the State of Luxemburg, while on my left was a vivacious young American with a Southern accent. Her eyes were a cornflower blue; her wrists delicately thin and one could see the clear blue veins run through the back of her hand, as she sketched idly but expertly on her copy of the overlarge, gold-framed, blue-printed menu. It was in fact a neat sketch of our hostess which provided the start for our conversation.

"My, isn't the major's wife pretty?" she enthused. "Do you know why I am here tonight in all this celebrated gathering of all you distinguished soldiers and civilians? Well, the major's wife and I travelled over to Cherbourg from New York together on the same boat. Can you imagine travelling five days together on the same boat and sharing one little cabin?"

I told her that I thought it might be a most enjoyable voyage.

"That's very gallant of you to say so, and very like a European. Americans would find that just a little naughty, but then Americans have such a highly developed Puritan background, don't you think?"

At this observation I thought I heard Angel sniff; and certainly she swung around in her chair a little more Luxemburg-wards.

I asked my companion her name. With a few strokes of her pencil she depicted on the menu a rosebud.

"Rose?"

"That's what my friends call me. But, of course, I don't know you well enough to know whether—" Her eyes flickered, as though for a fraction of a second a serious thought was in her mind; then she resumed her flirtatious play. "You Englishmen are so quick to flatter a girl and to make her feel that you've known her for years, when really we've only just met, haven't we? I don't think American men would dare to treat a girl so familiarly. Europeans are so gallant; my goodness, they make a simple American girl's head swim."

As she talked, in a kind of breathless drawl, she drew casually but rapidly a wicked caricature of Angel leaning her bosom heavily in the direction of her Luxemburg admirer. "You don't believe that I'm called Rose? Oh, how can you be so ungallant? Well, if you don't like Rose, I must think of some other name that will please you more. Perhaps Dorothy, that's a good English name. If you don't like Rose for my name, I guess I'll have to make an exception for you, and you may call me Dorothy."

All this while, Angel seemed to be getting on famously with the stout gentleman from Luxemburg. I could hear him expounding to her the beauties of his country and its capital city, and I thought I could detect snatches of conversation in which he was inviting her to take a weekend there and sample with him its joys and pleasures at first hand. The German waiters kept bringing us more champagne, and the major beamed over his happy international assembly, and Dorothy-Rose kept teasing me with her deep southern drawl and with her fluttery, flirtatious southern ways.

"Now, let me see if I can guess your rank. Three pips on your shoulder. Don't tell me, do let me guess. One for lootenant, two for captain, three for major. That's it." Her blue eyes gazed at me flatteringly. "My, you look so very military, major."

I explained, slowly and carefully, that I held the rank of captain, but she insisted on elevating me all the same.

"When I was travelling over to Cherbourg with the major's wife and we were being terribly seasick, we just never dreamed that because of that I would be sitting next to an English major here tonight. And you know we folk in the United States have such a peculiar idea about the English being reserved and aloof. But you're not reserved and aloof, are you, major?"

It was true. What with the champagne flowing like water and Angel flinging herself with gusto into her proposed

Luxemburg trip and above all the flattering attentions of Dorothy-Rose, I was losing any little reserve I had. Dorothy-Rose me kept hard at it trying to keep up with her chatter.

"Major, are English women as beautiful as we are told they are? Are they all as beautiful as your very attractive companion who seems to be so deeply involved with the stout gentleman from Luxemburg? Major, you must find American women very dull in comparison."

It was not until the brandy and cigar phase of the banquet that my glow of satisfaction was suddenly snuffed out. The major had got up to say a few words. He introduced his wife; he went on to talk about the building up of allied goodwill. A goodwill which extended to all nations whose representatives were gathered in that room tonight. As I looked round at them I could recognise the military attachés of Holland, Denmark, Norway; the Ministry official from Luxemburg; a French colonel, and two French civilians from the Ministry; a Belgian colonel; various high-ranking US officers, and a number of seemingly important guests of whose exact status or nationality I had no idea. The major now went on to suggest that it would indubitably increase our mutual understanding, fellowship and goodwill and add peace on earth, if a representative of each nation present were given the same opportunity which he himself at that moment had of standing up and speaking to us of his country's contribution to this great task of rebuilding the shattered world anew.

I had a horrified vision of myself speaking out for Great Britain and the news breaking upon the startled desk of my brigadier at the War Office. I called one of the waiters standing by for a quick brandy and while the military attaché of Norway began in heavy but professional style to deliver himself of a long and carefully worded statement, I tried to figure out what on earth to say when my turn came.

"My, isn't the Norwegian military attaché handsome?" wrote Dorothy-Rose on her menu and passed it to me. I pushed it back nervously.

"And such a witty speaker," she added in her neat hand. Desperately I tried to review all the things I might wittily—or unwittily—say; she scribbled on her menu yet again and pushed it under my anxious nose. It said, "I'm sure you will be wonderful, major, too."

No politics, I thought, I must keep off politics. Be uncontroversial. Seem to say something without in fact saying anything at all. Something different from the professional political speeches. Why, oh why had the major invited me? Instead of some suave diplomat whose job it was to handle such occasions? I looked to Angel for comfort and consolation, but Angel had turned her back on me.

I couldn't think of a thing, not a single thing. I remembered I had once heard of a man in a similar situation. When his turn came to speak he simply said, "I can't sing, I can't dance, I can't tell funny stories, but what I can do is give three hearty British cheers." This pathetic idea now lodged itself in my inebriated brain as the perfect solution. Three hearty British cheers for our host and his charming hostess. The whole round table would rise to a spontaneous tribute to the major and his wife; a gesture which would utterly dwarf all the previously uttered empty phrases; would be warm, sincere, moving. I sat back with relief, called for another brandy and wrote on Dorothy-Rose's overcrowded menu, beneath her remarks about the Norwegian: "Yes, but rather hackneyed political stuff, don't you think?"

The speeches moved round, until it was now the turn of the Belgian colonel. My turn would come when he had finished. He rose, a bluff red-faced old chap, a veteran of the war.

"I am a soldier," he barked, "not a politician. All I wish to say is that we should drink a toast to our 'ost and 'ostess." He paused and glared, with bloodshot eyes, around the table. "So, I ask you to give three hearty cheers for the major and his wife. 'Eep, 'eep-'eep, 'urr-rrah!"

As we drove away in the jeep afterwards, I remember Angel sulking furiously and then, amid the silence of the homeward journey, her cold and haughty voice saying, "I'm ashamed of you, I'm horribly ashamed. I never thought you could let England down so badly. And in front of all those foreigners. It was dreadful, absolutely dreadful—"

I was stung to the quick and the jeep rocked wildly over the cobbled road. I thought she was referring to the awfulness of my hastily improvised toast. But when she added, "I simply can't *stand* American women," I laughed with relief. What Angel didn't know was that in my pocket was Dorothy-Rose's menu card. "Well done, major," she had written teasingly, "and thanks for being such fun."

Perhaps the evening hadn't been a complete disaster after all.

XIII

There was the usual fog of smoke and babble of chatter over the clink of glasses. Most of all, a bewildering crowd of faces at this HQ party. A lot of top brass and their women were present, but no one I knew except my American colleague Loot. The pair of us stood around, feeling very junior indeed. It was a bad time for me. Angel and I had called it a day after the affair of the major's dinner party. And Zara had gone off with her Chief of Mission to some special posting in Paris. I couldn't have been more alone. I missed Zara. That's how it is after a war. Everybody on the move, nothing allowed to settle. Nothing you can do about it, but get on with the job and burn up time the best you can.

I could see Loot scanning the faces in the large salon, more in desperation than in hope. Then his eyes lit up and a mischievous grin twisted his mouth.

"Hey, man," he said. "There's Irene over there. She's a fellow countryman of yours."

We edged our way carefully to where she sat on a sofa, swathed in shimmering silk. She had green eyes and an oval face with a long, prominent nose. Skin, soft and supple: her dark hair swept back in a coil. Jade earrings. She was striking enough to make anyone gape. As I stood goofing at her, a little quiver ran down her nose; the green eyes searched me through. I nearly jumped out of my skin.

We talked for some time. She had a serpent-like quality

which made me feel as if green scaly coils were closing around me, and her nose-quiver seemed like some orgiastic shudder before she devoured her prey. She did not wish to join the dancers in the neighbouring room, but sat patiently on the sofa, inscrutable as Mona Lisa among the rocks, just sitting the party out; very proper, modest, withdrawn. When I asked if I could see her again, she shrugged and held herself aloof.

Afterwards I learned that she was a secretary to one of the colonels. Loot and the other younger officers were bitter about her because she would have nothing to do with anyone below the rank of colonel. They had nicknamed her 'Duchess'. "Watch out," said Loot, "Give her a wide berth. You'll never get a date with her. Leave her well alone."

It is a sad comment on human vanity that one always hopes to succeed where others have failed, and that good advice merely stirs up secret expectations. I rationalised that they had failed because they were Americans; I would succeed because I was English. I even took a small bet with Loot that I would get a date with her.

I tried finding a table near her in the cafeteria at breakfast time. I sent little friendly waves in her direction. She just got on with her doughnut and coffee, and read her air-mail edition of the *New York Herald Tribune*. I tried wandering into that part of the vast HQ building where she worked in an office largely made of glass; but she never looked up from her typing and all my efforts seemed doomed to failure.

Moreover, I was fully occupied with my share in the I&E inter-allied goodwill scheme. I hadn't been able to get any more British speakers to come over. As usual, the trouble was that all my reports and requests intended for the War Office had to go via BAOR. Carefully composed, painfully typed—Julie smiled at me now, but the old lady made sure she didn't do my typing—they came back, with comments such as 'Regret no', 'Too late', 'Where is the payment to come from?' and, above all, 'When are the Americans sending an officer in exchange to *us*?"

The inter-allied goodwill project seemed to be dying on its feet. The promised Russian speaker hadn't turned up, the French lieutenants had returned home. The major was going frantic.

"Why the hell can't we get any British speakers?" he demanded.

I explained to him about British military procedures—messages having to go via BAOR and all that.

"For crying out loud," he said. "You mean you just couldn't fly over to London and fetch us a speaker?"

"Colonel would have me court-martialled," I told him. "Probably shot at dawn."

The major goggled. "You could be in London in two hours," he urged. "Don't write. Just forget all that typing and think of the time you'll save. You fix it up in London for a speaker to come over direct to us. We pay his fee, we fly him over here, we travel him around. What's that got to do with your colonel?"

"By plane?" I said with astonishment.

"US army air force," said the major, "we can requisition you a seat on one of their planes any time. No problem."

I took him up on it. A couple of days in London seemed just the ticket. The major was rubbing his hands. "We'll cover for you," he assured me.

The trip was a great success. It worked out so well and seemed so simple that I began to take off just whenever I felt my work needed it. The Americans who knew about my visits, didn't query them; and the British who would have queried, didn't know.

It was fun flying home. I could get a plane early in the morning and have bacon and eggs in Frankfurt at seven, fly to Paris and lose an hour, eat another bacon and egg breakfast in the US canteen there, also at seven; reach Bovingdon Airport and, if my stomach could take it, have bacon and eggs there too.

At Bovingdon the customs officials were friendly and casual about my luggage. Although there was a good deal of smuggling going on, mainly in Swiss gold watches bought by servicemen on the black market, to me both the black market and smuggling were a mug's game. Virtue and indolence alike prevented me from attempting to bring into England a single item over the permitted allowance. It was no wonder that the customs people at Bovingdon used to wave me through like an old friend.

Amid all this journeying back and forth from Frankfurt to London, I did not forget Irene and my small bet with Loot. Nevertheless I had to admit that my attempts to make contact had now begun to peter out into routine gestures. Then one day she passed me in the cafeteria queue and gave me that green-eyed stare and that little nasal shudder which turned me on quite helplessly. When I approached her table, with my orange juice in one hand, a plate of waffle and syrup in the other, she not only smiled in reply to my 'Good morning' but invited me to sit down and have breakfast with her. We enjoyed each other's company so much that we were half an hour late for the office. I saw Loot glance questioningly at me as I came in.

"I've got a date," I bragged. "Tonight. At her apartment. That's a bottle of champagne you owe me, Loot."

"Yeah, I saw you. But watch her, boy. She's a boa-constrictor, that dame. She'll just eat you alive."

There were two other couples at Irene's flat that night, two English girls with steady American boy friends. From the record-player came soft lulling music; the only lights were table lamps. Irene lay curled up on the sofa, when she wasn't being hostess keeping an eye on everyone's drinks. Her cigarette in its holder gave off a red glow as she basked languidly on green velvet cushions. The steady couples kept nice and steady to themselves. That left Irene and me on the sofa.

We spent a good deal of time in what I suppose can only be called mutual admiration. Irene said she had heard about my work. "All those VIPs you're getting to come over to entertain the troops."

"Trying to get."

"But it's very clever of you, darling, and I hear you just fly off to London whenever you feel like it."

"I do *some* work here, you know."

"Yes, I know, darling, but you always seem to be flying off and disappearing on a sort of magic carpet, so that I've never really been able to get to know you. And now that we're just beginning to get acquainted I'll bet anything that you'll be off again."

"As a matter of fact," I answered modestly, "I'm off tomorrow."

"Tomorrow? How lucky you are. I'm dying to go home and see my parents in Newcastle. Do you know, it's ages since I last saw them. I write to them every week. But I feel so mean, living like a princess here while they have such a hard time of it in England. I tried to mail them presents, but so many used to arrive damaged or broken that they wrote to me and asked me not to send them any more."

Her green eyes had grown sad and tender.

"I've got a wonderful piece of Dresden china I bought for Mummy. You know what marvellous china you can get here in Germany. I saw it in Heidelberg and I just had to buy it. And, d'you know, now I've bought it I can't think how I'm going to get it back to Mummy. I shan't be going home on leave for *years*. So you see, I was silly really to get it, wasn't I?

"Quite, quite crazy," I said.

"You couldn't," she said, sitting up suddenly and looking right through me. "I suppose you couldn't... just possibly...no, of course, you couldn't."

The little shiver once again spread down her nostrils, her

green eyes smouldered; and the long jade earrings quivered like meadow grass.

It was late when I set off home, with the package under my arm, carrying it very carefully because Dresden is so fragile and Irene had warned me not to slip. She had kissed me goodnight most tenderly, so that I was quite giddy in the damp night air and held on tight to my neatly wrapped box of chinaware lest I should damage it.

However, it was no bother either then or next morning on the flight. At Bovingdon the customs people were as obliging as ever, and it was only a matter of minutes before I was comfortably settled in the bus from the airport to London. I had taken the package from my hand luggage and laid it on my lap so as to be quite sure that its contents would not come to harm. Moreover, the package lying snugly there reminded me of the soft warmth of Irene, of her melting goodnight kiss, and of the promise implied of many more wonderful evenings to come.

So, sweetly and pleasantly, we were moving along the few remaining miles to London, when we hit a stretch of road that obviously hadn't been repaired for years. The bus bounced like a plane on landing; the back of the seat hit my spine, my knees jerked up. Irene's present slid with a jolt to the floor.

As I reached to retrieve the package, I gave it an apprehensive shake. It felt loose, and in sudden panic I tugged at its covering paper.

I tore off the wrapping and lifted the cardboard lid. Then as I shuffled the tissue paper aside, there in the box the present lay, in a dozen separate pieces.

Each piece was worth its weight in gold: twelve Swiss watches smuggled in unwittingly—by an idiot.

XIV

Although Mollie and Michele were both typists working for the Americans in Frankfurt, they were not friends, indeed they may not even have known each other. I knew them both, though not with any special involvement.

Mollie was impulsive, easily agitated into words and action, and then as easily appalled by her own reckless acts. Michele was calm and thoughtful; she did not project herself into a gay off-duty life like Mollie, but found a quiet and domestic peace alone. There were other differences, but they are the trivial ones: physical appearance, for instance. Michele had dark hair, brown eyes, a finely chiselled nose; her face was poised and gentle. Mollie was tall, redheaded, blue-eyed, and freckled.

We were sitting one evening at a table in the darkened hall of the forces' club, watching one of the cabaret shows officially instituted for the troops. The show was pretty dreary, and Mollie was more interested in telling me her views of girls who ran after the American officers.

"I'm not an officers' tart," she said. Her Cockney vowels gave her voice a slight whine. "Just look at some of them putting on their airs, because they're ready to go to bed with the first Yank lootenant who takes them out and buys them a drink. I'm a sergeant's girl. You'll never catch me with an officer. Not that many of them haven't tried. Nothing doing."

"What about me?"

"Oh, you're different, you're British. You don't get their pay, now, do you? I bet you don't get paid any more than a Yankee sergeant."

"Less," I said.

"OK," said Mollie, "then I'm buying the next round of drinks."

She was a good kid, was Mollie. She hadn't been spoilt like the American officers' girls.

"It's all right," she went on, "I can afford it. Do you know how much we typists get paid here? Well, I mean, why do you think I'm here at all? Not because I like Germany, nor the lousy Yanks. Do you know I earn nearly four times what I'd get working in London? And I've gotta kid to keep. You didn't know I had a kid, did you? Lives with her gran in Battersea."

I glanced at the fingers of her left hand. She wasn't wearing her wedding ring.

She must have noticed my glance, for she said, "I'm separated from her father. Do you know, he hasn't contributed a penny since he went to Canada? He's a mean bastard."

Silently for a moment we watched a satin-clad chanteuse undulating round the microphone. "I got you under my skin," she warbled lugubriously, "...deep in the heart of me."

"Oh my Gawd," said Mollie. I thought she was going to burst into tears, but she turned her emotion into renewed verbal energy. "*He's* under my skin all right. Do you know, I'd leave here without even packing my things if he asked me to come back. I would that. Silly, isn't it, when he's left me, oh, it must be more than two years now, and I've been messing around with all these Yankee sergeants. *He* was a sergeant, you know. Now he's trying to divorce me, seems he's got another woman back in Canada he wants to marry. But if he asked me I'd go back to him tomorrow."

I didn't know much about Mollie except that lately she had been shacking up with an American sergeant called Van.

They went fairly steady together until one of their quarrels occurred, then they both went haywire for about a week. I guessed that this happened to be one of the times they had quarrelled.

"Men," she said, "they're all the same, aren't they? There's Van now, he's gone off on the razzle, running around with some fraulein—"

"Not Veronica Dankeschön?" I joked. Mollie gave me an unappreciative look.

Veronica Dankeschön was a strip-cartoon character featured in *Stars and Stripes,* the official newspaper of the US forces in Germany. Sophisticated, curvaceous, sexy and willing, she regularly brought about the downfall of some nice American boy too naive to see through her vampire designs. The troops took a natural interest in her adventures and in no time at all she became their favourite pin-up. This was not what the officials, who launched her, intended. She was intended rather to be a dreadful warning to young soldiers, the semi-clad Lorelei who lured them to their doom. The significant initials of her name were embroidered on her panties or other convenient underclothing, which the cartoonist so regularly displayed.

The cabaret too that we were watching was part of the big drive to keep the boys off the streets where the frauleins were. The orchestra was a group of five sad middle-aged musicians. The German dancing girls were older and plumper versions of Veronica D. middle-aged blondes with rolling eyes, rolling breasts, swaying hips, suggestive hands.

"Terrible about this VD, isn't it," Mollie chattered on. "Van says that four soldiers out of every five catch it. Do you really think it's that bad? I mean, it'd be awful if it was right, wouldn't it? Well, just look around and think that if four out of every five men here—It fair turns your stomach over, doesn't it?"

There was a pause, then she said, "I wonder if Van's all

right? You know, Van and I see a lot of each other, but some-times he goes off with the frauleins. They're the ones who spread it among the boys and the boys pass it on to the decent girls like us. I tell you, it's a rotten world, isn't it? After all, I came over here to earn some money, not to catch a dose of VD."

"Maybe he's the lucky fifth man," I suggested flippantly.

She gave me the look my remark deserved. "If it wasn't for that husband of mine I wouldn't have to do this. You'da thought he would have sent me some money to support the kid." She went quiet for a moment. "I'm not pretending I was perfect." Then tears came into her eyes. "Oh God, do you know, I'd go back to him tomorrow if he'd give me the chance."

"How do you know he won't?"

"Oh, God, I know he won't."

"Have you ever asked him?"

She looked at me in amazement, as if the idea had taken her breath away.

"No, I couldn't do that. I couldn't think of that."

"Well, why not? You've changed your mind about him in the two years since you saw him last. Perhaps he has changed too? Maybe he's wishing he was back with you, like you're wishing to be with him."

"God almighty, do you really think so?"

"Maybe he's wishing you'd ask him to take you back, just waiting for you to ask him."

"Christ!" She sat there, just staring, too overcome to say anything.

"Come on," I said. "Come on, let's go and see if we can book a phone call to Canada."

"To Canada? To Winnipeg? Will he be in, do you think? Will I be able to talk to him? What shall I say? Oh, my God, what shall I say?"

We were lucky with the operator and the connection to Canada was made with only a short delay. Mollie sat nervously twisting her already grubby little handkerchief in her red-freckled hands. She seemed suddenly a little child again and I could imagine her baby growing up just like her.

When the Winnipeg number came through I told her to make sure that she really gave him the works, no false pride etc. Then I disappeared and left her to it. As I went through the door I could hear that downbeat whine come into her voice again.

"Is that you, Al? This is your wife, Mollie, Al. I'm ringing you because I love you. I want you to come back, Al."

Somehow it didn't sound hopeful. There were long pauses and she spoke without conviction as though the man at the other end was being brutal to her. I imagined him being woken out of bed, red-eyed and nerves jagged. It occurred to me that if Al was on the point of divorcing Mollie and remarrying some Canadian girl, he wouldn't be very pleased about this development at all. I realised that we had been drinking a bit too convivially at the club and that the whole idea was absurdly sentimental.

Like two people who had exposed each other's crucial weakness, Mollie and I kept apart after that failure of her telephone attempt to win back Al. Not seeing her during the next week or so in any of her favourite haunts, I guessed that she and Van must have made it up, once Van had had his fling.

Meanwhile the big VD campaign went on. In the *Stars and Stripes* editorials, articles, graphs, and statistics kept appearing daily. There were lectures, and discussions within the units. It soon became the No. 1 topic of conversation, and as the campaign steamed ahead to scare the troops, you could see a lot of white faces in the queue at the Medical Officer's each morning. All the empty, alien feelings of living in an occupied country were intensified by this spreading fear.

It was to escape such an atmosphere that I decided to visit

Michele. A Sunday visit to her flat had always been a source of quiet and peaceful pleasure, and I had not seen her for some weeks. She cooked her own meals, with typical Parisienne excellence, made her place a little artistic oasis in that desert of foreign-occupied land, and lived a self-contained and peaceful life which had its own charm. Secure in her neat and elegantly ordered room, we enjoyed discussing books, listened to classical music, and talked a little gossip. For Michele it was a life lived as much as possible like that she would have lived in Paris. Except that she was lonely, though how lonely I had not realised.

She was a girl not given to undue demonstration of her feelings, so I was taken by surprise when she opened the door and flung her arms around me.

"I'm so glad to see you," she said, "I need a friend," and began to weep.

"Michele, what is it?"

"I'm sorry," she said, "for being so sentimental." Her smile wavered like a reflection in a steamed-up mirror.

"It is nothing," she said, moving away so that I could not see her face. "I've been a fool."

Cherchez l'homme, I thought—but this time, I warned myself, no interference. No phone calls, no boy scout act, no involvement.

"I've been so unhappy here in Germany. I don't like the Germans and I don't like the Americans—"

"But the British are all right?"

She gave me a fleeting smile.

"The British are all right. But there are not any other French girls that I know. And so I have been very lonely."

"I'm sure there are plenty of men who—"

"I despise the girls here who go and sleep with men they don't really love. Yes, I despise them."

After a while she added, "I don't know why I did it, except that this man seemed kind to me at work. I don't know why,

131

except I was lonely."

She ended there, as though a kind of stubborn distrust had thrust itself between us.

It took a long time before the distrust crumbled, so that when it did her words fell like pebbles dropped into a deep well.

"I think he's got VD."

Next day I took her along to the MO. Early, before work and before the queue formed. She had dressed herself, as she always did, very smartly, very neatly; with taste.

When she went in to see the doc, I sat there on the waiting-room bench. It was a bare room—four plain wooden walls, a few long benches, a battered green bin marked 'WASTE', and a heavy-built table on which lay a pile of grubby periodicals and papers. From the well-thumbed pile I picked up a copy of the *Stars and Stripes* and idly turned the pages, wondering how Veronica Dankeschön was getting on in her scheme to seduce the US Army single-handed.

"My God," exclaimed a white-faced redhead, "what are you doing here?" She was only a shade of the full-blooded Mollie I had last seen. "Not you too?"

I stared at her uncomprehendingly.

"You haven't got it too, have you? VD, I mean."

I shook my head, but she didn't pay much attention to me; she was too absorbed in her own worries.

"It's Van," she moaned. "He's been with some fraulein. I think I've picked it up from him. You know, I don't care any more. If Al divorced me I was going to marry Van. Now I just don't care."

There was a long silence. I remembered how she had twisted and untwisted her handkerchief when I was fixing the call to Canada for her. Then suddenly she looked up at me and glared sulkily.

"Well, say something, can't you?"

Outside the window there was bright morning sunshine. A group of denimed soldiers were laughing as they traced out in the morning paper the latest instalment of the strip cartoon; their sudden male laughter seemed to split the sky-blue surface of the air.

Mollie was sitting on the wooden bench, her pale eyes shone with anger.

"Men," she said. "I hate them."

XV

"Say, Cap. Any news about when your colonel is coming yet?"

The major used to ask this question every morning as he sat at his desk, blinking through his thick Army-issue spectacles, watching me open my mail from BAOR. He attached great, almost obsessional importance to the idea of my colonel's reply to the invitation to meet his own CO in Frankfurt.

"Nothing in the mail," I reported cheerfully.

"Maybe you and I ought to take off for a quick trip up there to find out what's the snag. I'd sure like to know what's fouling things up. Along the autobahn," the major murmured dreamily, "in the sun."

"As far as Kassel; then you're in the British Zone, where it's all cobbled road and country lanes. A rotten road for swanning."

"We *must* get him," said the major, "my colonel won't move without him. Maybe if you phoned—"

"Oh God, no," I cried, "he hates the telephone."

I had seen it happen. When the call came through for him, he would pick up the instrument and gradually entangling himself with cable, would turn round glaringly and bark at us, "Well, how do you use this damn thing? Do *you* know how it works? Who the hell knows how this thing works? Well, don't *any* of you know?"

And while we all stood fascinated and tongue-tied, he

would bang it on the desk or table or against the wall. "There, that's better. No, the damn thing still won't work." Then he would bash it up and down several times more, finally replace it on the hook and looking at us say, "Lot of nonsense. Probably not important, eh?" and go huffing out.

I could still recall how on my return from Berlin he had gone on about my posting being the most iniquitous thing he had ever known happen in the whole of his serving career; that this was what was happening in these modern, peacetime days; that he didn't know what the War Office was up to. Nobody was shorter of officers than he was; officers were being filched from him daily. If the War House wanted officerless troops and chaos in the Army this was the way to go about it. He had not been consulted, and if he had been consulted he would never have recommended it, in fact, he would have done his damn well best to prevent it. He didn't want to set eyes on me again either in the office or out of it and I could go to blazes for all he cared.

It was a shock therefore to find one day a telecom from BAOR stating that the colonel intended to accept the Americans' invitation.

The major was cock-ahooping with delight. "Boy, this will make things hum. Wait till we get him and my chief together. Yessir, we're on the move at last."

I wasn't so happy; but I couldn't tell the major that our colonel didn't care a damn for Anglo-American relations, he only wanted to see if he could find a way to get his officer back. Still, I tried to make the best of things by suggesting to myself that maybe lavish hospitality and a friendly reception by the Americans might placate him.

The major rushed about enthusiastically. "The VIP treatment. We *must* give him the VIP treatment," he chanted, until it began to sound like a magic spell that would solve everything. "Courtesy call on the CO. Dinner at the hotel. Quiet night's rest. Next day when he's freshened up, we'll lay on visits, discussions, demonstrations and show him what we're doing in this goodwill job. Then when he begins to see the range and scope of our activities,"—the major made the word 'scope' sound somehow vast and global—"we'll work on him with our future plans for zonal interchange of personnel, but on a big scale. Yessir—" the major was off on his dream, his eyes blinking excitedly.

On the day itself we waited expectantly at the office for his arrival due at late afternoon. One hour went by, then two. The major begun cracking his knuckles nervously, behind the edge of his desk.

"Say," he blinked, "I thought these guys in the British Army made a big thing of their punctuality. And all that stuff." His knowledge of Britain was mainly derived from films and he attributed to Britons all kinds of mystical and mysterious virtues.

I reminded him once again of the bad state of the cobbled roads in the British Zone.

"That's right," said Loot, remembering our journey there.

The major cracked a knuckle and pointed out that by this time he ought to be on the autobahn in the American Zone, where *nothing* could go wrong. I was just retorting that with this man and something mechanical like a car, *anything* could happen, when we saw him arriving. Arriving is the wrong word. He burst upon us like a bomb.

"Young man," he roared, "find me your American colonel." It seemed that after travelling out of the British Zone, he had stopped at an American forces' vehicle-servicing station on the autobahn and demanded petrol. The American sergeant in charge of the station insisted that he had no authority to supply gasoline to anybody except American personnel. The colonel counter-insisted that (a) he was a colonel, (b) British, (c) on a goodwill visit to the American forces and (d) at their own blasted invitation.

He had only made the journey, he raged, in order to suggest

that I should pack up this damn nonsense I was doing in Frankfurt and come back with him and do a worthwhile job in an efficiently run army, but one which was suffering an acute officer shortage, so that if we didn't look out we would end up as damn inefficient as the Yanks themselves. Then, turning to glare at the major whose presence he seemed to recognise for the first time, he shouted at me, "If the bloody Yanks won't agree to your return, then I'm going to have my pound of flesh, by God, and take an American officer back in exchange. Now, where's this American colonel?"

I escorted him to the building and he seemed quite calm again.

"Wow," said the major when I got back, "I sure wouldn't like to have that guy breathing down my neck twenty four hours a day."

"It was your colonel asked for him to come," I pointed out, "maybe your colonel can calm him down."

What exactly passed at the interview I never knew. But his American counterpart was a fine old fighting soldier, like himself. And certainly the colonel came out after about an hour's private conference almost jocular. Indeed several times I caught him looking at me rather thoughtfully as I took him in his car to the hotel. I took him into the comfortable lounge, saw that he had a whiskey and soda inside him, instructed the waiter to keep his glass filled, and with much relief began to take my leave.

"Oh, by the way," he said, "your American colonel and I quite agree about the problem of officer exchange. I think we shall find a way of overcoming it. Goodnight."

I didn't like the confident and easy way he said it. I could detect a special gleam in his eye as he looked at me that seemed to spell an almost proprietorial interest. It seemed only too clear that the American colonel had given in to his obsessional demand that he should be allowed his officer back.

When I arrived anxiously at the office early next morning, I was greeted by the major.

"Hey, Cap. You've been wanted on the phone," he stuttered, "your colonel's been phoning you ever since the crack of dawn. There's a message to report to his hotel at once."

Outside the imposing portico of the hotel, the colonel, in his hat and greatcoat, was pacing up and down the street like a tiger on parade. His car was parked by the kerb with his driver in attendance, and the engine running.

"By God, young fellow," he exclaimed, "do you realise what you've done? This hotel—" and he nearly choked on the words—"this hotel is a nightmare. Do you realise I've not slept all night? Is this how you look after your senior officer? Tell me, is this how you always carry out your duties or is this special to me?"

"It's the best hotel in Frankfurt, sir," I stammered.

"The best hotel!" He exploded so violently that for some seconds words failed him. "That room where I slept—was supposed to sleep, that is,—do you know it is nothing better than a box room? Do you know that, eh? Do you?"

I didn't, of course.

"Do you know that there was so much racket with drunken American troops in the bar lounge until three o'clock in the morning, that I couldn't go to sleep, no ordinary person could have gone to sleep, do you know that? Do you?"

I didn't know that, either.

"Do you know what that fool of a hotel manager said when I complained? No, I won't tell you that. Three o'clock, young man, before that racket died away. Do you know what I'd do with any of my officers who behaved like that? Do you?"

I was pretty sure I knew.

"And that's not all. At three o'clock the lift began working; next door to my room, the room you chose for me. Men going up and down like jack-in-the-boxes. And women. German women. Disgusting. Did you know that, eh? There ought to be a full report on this to the general commanding, and—" he added significantly, glowering at me— "to the War Office."

"Then what else do you think your brilliant arrangements had in store for me? Have you ever slept over the hotel kitchen? No, of course you haven't. But you put me over one. Have you ever heard them emptying the pans? Banging the meat? Clearing the dishes? Singing, bawling, whistling, beating accompaniment with their confounded spoons and pots and pans."

He paused to glare at me and the red knobbles on his cheeks seemed to glow until they reached the bloodshot in his eyes.

He turned on his heel and took three or four steps to the car. The driver sprang into ramrod-like mechanical life, the door was opened and shut; the driver sprinted back into the driver's seat, the engine still running.

I suppose it was a couple of hours later that back in the office the major picked up the phone. At first he looked astounded, then he began to blink.

"Hey, Cap. Your colonel's on the phone. He's stuck at that service station again. Something about the sergeant won't let him fill up his tank with gasoline. He says we'd better fix it for him quick."

He listened for a few minutes, helplessly fascinated by the flow of language.

"Or else," he added weakly, and put the phone down.

Of course, the colonel got his gasoline. He got his officer, too— but it wasn't me. Things like the hotel arrangements and then the gasoline may have helped to cool his desire to have me back in his HQ. I was very relieved about that.

But it was sad saying goodbye to the major a few days later. He was blinking very nervously as he set out to his new goodwill exchange posting in BAOR, arranged by his colonel and mine.

XVI

It is not easy, even after all these years, for me to write about Lilli.

She organised concerts for the American forces at a cultural club in Frankfurt. I met her during my visit to make arrangements for the booking at the Club of an English pianist on a goodwill tour. From the beginning I knew she was different from the other women I had met in Germany. There had been others who had warmth and charm, yet with Lilli I instinctively felt that despite these qualities there was a hidden secret, a dark shadow, something sombre and even shocking perhaps.

Our shared interest in music and literature drew us together and, sitting in her comfortable, almost luxuriously furnished office, we talked long after we had completed our plans for the piano recital. It became clear too that she was a first rate organiser of cultural activities.

"Would you like to come to tonight's concert?" she asked. Her eyes were brown, warm, earthy, like the sun on ploughed land; her hair black and shoulder length. She wore a bright red blouse with sleeves buttoned at the wrist. I do not remember her skirt, only the blood-red blouse with pearl buttons on the cuffs and front.

From a box in the concert hall we watched as violinist and pianist performed. On the stage below us the black lacquered piano gleamed like a shining shadow. The audience sat totally intent. Some appeared alert to the dangers of the musical tightrope which the performers walked, waiting critically for the first sign of a slip. Others held less tension in their bodies—something of them seemed to go out to the performers; they were at their ease. Some gazed at the performers, fascinated by their manual dexterity, as one might watch light-fingered jugglers; others closed their eyes, shuttering out all except the pure and liquid sounds which came to them in the darkness.

A young couple were holding hands. Their bodies leaned towards each other; it seemed as though a great joy and a great sadness filled them. On stage you could see the violinist's changing facial expressions and grimaces, and the fluttering of his thinning hair. But the stillness of the two lovers was as if they were a painting, a sculpture, or the detail from a frieze. I took Lilli's hand in mine. She hardly seemed aware, and yet even the calm stillness of her palm sent a message impossible to misread.

We went back to her flat, still in that dreamlike mood that music sometimes creates. In the flat the long curtains were drawn as if to enclose us in a world within the world; they were splashed with patterns of primitive red and green, vivid and Gauguinesque. Within the spacious living room the arrangement of the furniture seemed to curve around us in an embrace of its own.

One item alone broke this harmony. On the central mantelpiece stood a rectangular greenish-tinted glass tank, covered by a sliding lid into which ventilation slats were fitted.

"That is my reptarium," she smiled, handing me a drink. "Do you like it?"

A lazy-looking snake coiled itself behind the glass as if it knew we were inspecting it, and slowly turned its unblinking face towards my gaze.

"I call him Peter," she murmured. "He often sleeps in bed

with me." Seeing my startled look, she added, "Oh, he is quite harmless. He likes the warmth of my body. And I like to feel his cool skin as he crawls close to me in bed and coils around me. It is a very pleasant sensation. Don't you like snakes?"

"Not in bed," I said and quickly looked away from the cold-eyed creature. On the mantelpiece beside the reptarium lay an opened volume of Baudelaire's poems. I picked up the book and glanced at it. It was open at a poem called *Les Bijoux,* and the poem's rich, exotic, overheated language held my fascinated attention. It seemed to say something to me of Lilli which I found both exciting and troubling.

Looking up, I saw Lilli watching me with a smile that was half-mocking. "He is a true poet," she said and took me by the hand, drawing me away from Peter and from Baudelaire. It was as if I had been put to some sort of test, and though I had failed she was not rejecting me.

We finished our drinks. I was silent and I thought Lilli sensed my unease. "Tonight," she said, "I shall have no need of Peter." As she spoke she smiled with such a particular sweetness that I had a sudden vision of her as Vivien, the Arthurian temptress whose beauty had seduced Merlin even though he knew her to be a witch.

Taking my hand in hers, she led me to her bedroom: it was cool, and elegant. A tall standard lamp was its sole illumination. The double bed was large and its sheets fresh and white. "I shall switch off the light," Lilli said, "we can undress in the dark." I was under her spell, like one who moved in a dream.

There was a faint glow in the room from the lightly curtained window. It was enough only to show the pale glimmer of our almost ghostly bodies. Lilli was the first into bed and pulled the sheets over her. As I climbed in beside her I was aware of the luminous whiteness of her face, beside which her hair, eyes, even her lips were black voids, like the dark air around us. The vision seemed intangible, of strange and almost mystical beauty. But her body was cool and real and her lips met mine in calm, untroubled relaxation.

In this mood she lay passive as if waiting for me to catch fire. I hesitated: was this how she lay when Peter writhed and coiled himself about her? She let me kiss and stroke her, barely moving with each caress. She was neither frigid nor unwilling to respond to my movements, yet clearly they did not excite her. I was aware of an emptiness, for which I could find no reason. I began to feel tired and felt a great desire to sleep, but as I rolled drowsily onto my back, Lilli leaned over me, her breasts lightly touching the skin of my chest.

"You thought it would be easy, didn't you?" she challenged. "You were wrong."

She placed my hand on her nipple. "Press it," she urged. "Hard."

Sleepily, I tried to tighten my grasp. "That is not hard enough, harder. I want you to *hurt* me."

Her tone was half-peremptory, half-pleading. As I responded she made a small involuntary convulsive movement. I knew she was speaking the truth. I exerted all the force in my finger and thumb and I could feel her loins begin to thrash.

"Better," she gasped. Suddenly she dived her hand under the pillow and brought out two small objects which she put into my hand; they felt like clips.

"One on each nipple," she urged. "Please," she said sharply. Then she said again "please," this time with a sort of desperate agony.

I obeyed.

"Now," she said. "Now you can try again to make love."

"Oh God," I said helplessly. "Is this what you really want?"

She reacted angrily. "Yes," she said, "I suppose it is a shock for a good, clean young English officer. Let me tell you though. I have lived through years that you have never known. Did you ever see the concentration camps?"

"No," I confessed. "I came to Germany too late, when the

143

war was over."

"No, you did not see the concentration camps, you did not see the few who survived, all skin and bones, and maimed for life. And you did not know that I am one of those. Yes, I was released when the US soldiers came, and I survived. But no one survived the concentration camps without being maimed in some way."

"But you are not maimed," I said. I had seen no signs of it, and I was torn between belief and disbelief. As if she sensed my doubt, she dived her hand under her pillow again and drew out something which by its thick handle and tapering cord I could feel to be a whip or switch.

"Use it," she demanded. "Here on my nipples." She rolled back onto the sheet and the pale ghostly shape of her breasts could just be discerned amid the dark.

"Are you afraid?" she taunted. I flicked at her tentatively, and she flung herself on me with a passion so powerful that I wanted to please and satisfy her in any way I could.

"Yes," she said, "Yes," rolling over. "Now, across my buttocks."

Each stroke of the whip on her buttocks seemed to sting me too—unbearably. Clumsy as my efforts were, she grew wildly excited. When her excitement reached its climax, she lay sobbing gently for a few moments. I think we both fell asleep.

We did not sleep long, did not enjoy a deep slumber; she stirred restlessly in my arms and we lay drowsily comforting one another for the humiliation we each had suffered. Several times in the night she disturbed me as her sleeping body twitched convulsively. Once she awoke and clutching me, murmured "Is it morning? In the morning don't—" She fell silent and I thought that she might have fallen asleep again.

"In the morning, Lilli, don't what?"

She stirred herself enough to say, "In the morning when you leave, don't switch the light on, and don't look at me."

"I can't promise that," I said lightly, "I'd like to see your face again before I go, your real face. Am I to remember you only as a phantom of the night?"

"Do as I ask," she said. "Please." There was an urgency in her tone that I did not understand.

"Why do you ask this, Lilli? What are you trying to say? Give me a reason."

She was fully awake now, lifting her shoulders from the bed. "All right, if you must have a reason, you shall have one. It is a long story, and you must hear it to the end."

"In the concentration camp there were Nazi doctors who experimented on the girls. First they experimented to see how much pain we could bear while they stimulated us sexually. They put clips on our bodies. Yes," she said in answer to my unspoken question, "on our nipples. We resisted their attempts to excite us, of course. This was possible because we hated them so for what they were doing to us. Everything died within us. That was the worst thing, to know we had no hope, no desire, only to endure from day to day what mad things they were doing to their human guinea pigs. They were mad—and so cold. I used to look at my captors to see if I could find any trace of a forgotten humanity within them. I could not understand how men might live without any human feelings whatever.

"Then one day when I was waiting my turn in the experiment room I was aware that we had a new German doctor. Just when I had given up all hope or desire to live, the eyes of this new doctor showed that he thought of me, he wanted to think of me, as human, as just a little bit more than an object of experiment. I could tell he was wavering inside his heart, even though he went through the torture programme and hurt me. Against my will I knew my eyes, my body were all pleading with him, were trying secretly to possess this small grain of humanity which I craved. All I wanted was for him just once to be human. One day he leaned over and touched me very gently. It was no longer an experiment, it was real, a touch of kindness. It was as though—as though he had forgotten himself, and was apologising with his finger tips."

"Oh Lilli," I murmured. She placed her fingers over my lips to halt my words.

"They took me away from the psychological section, perhaps it was a punishment for my making him so weak, and sent me to the medical experimentation unit, where they anaesthetised first my back, then other parts of my body, and they stripped sections of my skin. One time my back, between my shoulder blades; one time my thighs, another time around my waist. Each time the flesh had to heal and new tissue grow. Mine was good skin so they kept me alive while I had any left. Now my body is all scarred, and has no beauty, and I cannot love except through pain."

She was weeping so quietly that I wanted to feel the splash of her tears to assure me that I was not imagining it; but her weeping was tearless.

"You're still beautiful," I whispered desperately.

"No one knows my ugliness, but you. And even you will not really know, if in the morning you do not put on the light or draw back the sheets."

"I promise," I said, "word of an Englishman."

"An officer and a gentleman," she smiled, or so I thought. And that was my last thought, me half pompous, her voice half mocking, before sleep flicked off all further consciousness.

I awoke in the faint morning light. Lilli slumbered beside me, her soft features relaxed in deep sleep. Her hair lay black on the pillow. The white sheet covered her to her chin. One arm had been thrown over the sheet and lay outstretched, shapely from wrist to shoulder.

I didn't switch on the light as I got up and dressed, but I opened the long curtain just a few inches to help me find the bits and pieces of my clothes and army uniform. In the streak of early morning light which threw itself from curtain to bed I caught a second glimpse of Lilli's outstretched arm. Like a piece of mass-produced machinery or like a packaged crate for export, it carried its identity mark in crude blue figures. Tattooed along the length of the forearm was her concentration camp number 927051.

As I tiptoed out into the lounge, Peter rustled in his tank, baleful, sinister. Leaving her apartment, I was filled with a sense of shame. Those numerals tattooed on a human arm kept slanting across my vision as symbols of an obscenity too great for me to wish to remember. And somehow I too felt guilty.

XVII

It was a bit crazy. Here I was in London, courtesy of US Army air force, when I was supposed to be in Frankfurt. I was contacting civilian organisations, when I was supposed to be serving in, with, through, and for the army, in order to find speakers to represent the British Way of Life to US forces in Germany. Neither Colonel Furze nor the War Office knew what I was up to. But at least I was trying to get something done.

I was lucky that I could stay on these occasions with my cousin Giles at his flat overlooking the Vale of Health in Hampstead. My cousin was a good natured, gangling 6ft 6in man, who was a pacifist on political rather than religious or moral grounds. His wife had left him for a Yank officer at some stage during the war. Her desertion had hit him hard; nor had it been easy being a pacifist in wartime. He felt cut off and as we'd grown up very close anyway he liked to have me visit him. Especially as I could bring my American PX rations to London with me.

Ever since I told him about the girl who'd climbed through the bedroom window during my early days in Hoechst, he seemed to think that army life overseas was one long round of sexual activity. "Well," he'd begin, rubbing his hands, "have you had any more interesting adventures lately?"

I shook my head. Something was holding me back. It was as if this time—after Lilli—I wanted to forget such things.

"What about yourself?" I asked.

"All the girls love a soldier," he mocked, "not a bloody pacifist like me."

"In Germany it's not the uniform, it's the free cigarettes that matter," I said to encourage him. "Two for a short time, five for a long session, and ten all night—in fact all weekend if you wished. You should have joined the army, Giles," I teased.

"Shit the army," he said.

I told him about Johnny and the small fortune he was making from black marketing— "He's just a minor figure, though," I explained, "an amateur. It's the civvies who've created it, it's their way of surviving."

"I don't know why you work your butt off," Giles commented, "trying to make sense of the army and its stupid Occupation. Haven't you found yourself a decent girlfriend to settle with?" His question had a wishful, plaintive note. I reckoned he was asking about himself rather than me.

"There was a Hungarian girl called Zara—"

"What happened to her?"

"She got posted somewhere else."

"Since then?"

"The rest were pretty casual." Then I remembered what I was trying to forget and told him about Lilli.

"Bastards," he said.

"It's put me off casual affairs, I think."

"I *think* ?" echoed my cousin.

I hesitated a moment, surprised. "I must be settling down," I said. "Getting in practice for demob and back to normality again."

"Oh, come on," he laughed, "don't deprive me of any more of your comic adventures."

"And what about you?" I asked, "it's your turn now."

His face went blank, an almost agonised white. "Shit the rotten war," he said. "It's screwed all our lives up."

149

Although I'd by-passed BAOR I now found myself faced with civilian bureaucracy instead. I hawked my ideas for building Anglo-American goodwill in Germany from organisation to organisation: English Speaking Union, Tourist Board, British Council, Foreign Office, Ministry of Information. I had lots of talks, a few lunches, and the people I talked to were charming, sympathetic, and gave an appearance of being anxious to help. The Tourist Board seemed especially keen. But somehow things never quite came together. What I wanted always seemed to fall just outside their province.

The Ministry of Information had expressed interest, but immediately found a demarcation problem: should service to the American forces in Germany come under their American Division or under their European Division? In the end it seemed to come under neither. They were awfully sorry, but they themselves wouldn't after all be able to do anything. Perhaps the Foreign Office might be interested?

Next morning, back at the Hampstead flat, the telephone rang. Somebody from the Foreign Office wished to know if I could address an informal little meeting which they were arranging in a few days' time. Their object was to discuss how to develop inter-allied goodwill, the very problem I had been trying to interest so many worthy bodies in. I cancelled my flight back and decided that the age of miracles still lived on. Somebody had moved fast.

At the Foreign Office I was shown into a vast and gloomy building, along an avenue of corridors, and ushered into an office in which the furniture was heavy and upholstered in dark brown. Amid the air of deathly stillness in the ill-lit room I could hear a clock tick slowly. At one side of a large desk sat a young man with curly dark hair, writing out his reports. He introduced himself to me as Guy. His name I gathered later was Burgess. He was a friendly, lively man, and he introduced me to a colleague over from America whose name I did not catch. Burgess told me that the Foreign Office was interested in all efforts to promote Anglo-American-Soviet relations. "You did say the Soviets were included in your Allied liaison plans, didn't you?"

"The Soviets have been invited," I explained, "but we're still waiting for them to send us a liaison officer. Can't get a reply from them. Neither 'yes' nor 'no'."

"Not easy for them, old boy," said the tall slim fellow from Washington. "Very short of officers. Demob and all that."

"Sounds like our lot in BAOR," I ventured.

"Hm, yes. Well," Burgess continued, "we want to bring together all who might be interested in forming a committee for the purpose of co-ordinating attempts to promote Anglo-American-Soviet relations. And this is where you come in, since you've actually had some experience of this kind with the forces in Germany." He hoped I would take part in the discussion and perhaps say a few words about how the good-will scheme was working in Frankfurt.

So I settled down in a huge brown leather armchair to watch the various invited representatives arrive. Some of them I had met already on my visits to their organisations.

The last to arrive, and we seemed to have been waiting for him for some minutes after everyone else, was a military gentleman wearing a general's red cap band and red shoulder tabs. A brisk, intelligent-looking man in his late forties, with a neat haircut and moustache. With a start of alarm I realised that he must be my new general from the War Office. Interesting though it might be to see the features of the man to whom I had been sending my monthly reports, I had reported to him neither my arrival in London, nor its pur-pose, nor my doings since my arrival. As far as he knew I was safely in Frankfurt; in fact I was AWOL. I sank deeply into my armchair, making myself quite small and pretending that I really wasn't there.

Unfortunately, I wasn't allowed to sink into either nonentity or oblivion. For Guy was on his feet explaining to everybody the reason why he and his colleague had called this meeting. All those present were active in doing work of various kinds in relation to US troops in Germany or in building up inter-allied goodwill— British, American, French, and not forgetting the Soviets. But now they had the unusual opportunity of being able to learn from a British officer who had firsthand experience of the problem and who had kindly volunteered to attend this afternoon and would give them the benefit of his experience.

As I came out front to face my audience, I was aware that the general was staring straight ahead with tightly clamped jaw. He stared right through me to the wall behind while I tried to produce all this knowledge and experience with which I was supposed to edify them.

I did my best to explain the American GI's attitude towards his British allies. How he arrived in Britain expecting similarities and found differences, and I stressed the importance of these GIs returning to the US with a positive pro-British attitude. How each returning US 'veteran' would be the centre of local interest that was without parallel in our own country. Any pro-British or anti-British tendency on the part of returning US troops, therefore, could extend to many millions of American citizens back in the States. I could see the Foreign Office boys purring with pleasure at this introduction to the subject.

At the same time, I ploughed on, the GIs were sufficiently conscious that Europe had much to offer that was of interest and value. One day they would return with their wives and families to vacation among us, and as tourists their influence on the national exchequer would not be inconsiderable. Looking past my general I could see the Tourist Board people purring too.

But, I warned, we were up against a certain amount of 'competition' if that was the right word, from other countries which had been quick to see the national advantage that might be gained in this sphere, so that we needed to take decisive action while we still held a slight advantage.

There was a great deal more in this vein. Real politician's stuff, as I supposed. The upshot was that I was asked a lot of questions by everyone present (except my general who still seemed to be regarding the far wall with more interest). It was agreed by all (the general abstaining) to set up a co-ordinating committee. The chairman thanked me fulsomely for my inspiring address. Everyone applauded, except the general. I thought he might say something—unpleasant, of course—as we made our way out. But not a word, not a flicker of a sign of recognition.

When I got back to Hampstead my cousin said "There's been a telephone call for you."

"I know, from the War Office. The general's compliments and will I report to him immediately."

"Oh, did you know?"

"No," I answered, turning to go out of the door through which I had just entered, "but I could guess."

After all I had seen his grim, unsmiling face all afternoon.

"Well," he said in his soft slow voice—generals were always so smooth, they never barked like colonels or majors. "Well?"

"I'm sorry about this afternoon," I began.

"Look here, young man. I do not expect to find my junior officers putting me in a position where I might look ignorant or foolish."

"No, sir."

"I do not expect to find them absent from the place to which they have been posted, and for whatever reason present somewhere else without authorisation."

"No, sir."

"I do not expect to find them on my own doorstep in London without first having reported to me the nature of their mission."

He paused for my response.

"No, sir."

"Or stirring up civilian organisations, least of all without putting me in the picture."

"No, sir."

"Or addressing meetings at which I am invited to sit and listen to you lecturing me."

"No, sir."

"Especially when I haven't any knowledge of your arrival in London, nor what you've been up to these past weeks, nor what you might be going to suggest these organisations should do. In future, you will send a written report of your activities each month direct to me at the War Office."

"Yes, sir." I didn't tell him I had already been sending a monthly written report. I guessed he'd had enough trouble with the colonel in BAOR as it was.

"And should you ever need to re-appear in London with my permission you will take good care to report to me personally immediately upon your arrival. Moreover, you will consult me in future before you contact the heads of any civilian organisations. Your job is to see what can be done within the army, not outside of it."

"Yes, sir."

"And now, young man," said the general, suddenly relaxing and taking out his pipe, "do you smoke?" He passed me the silver cigarette box on his desk. "So tell me all about your difficulties."

I told him. About the major, and having to beg the Americans for transport every time I wanted to go anywhere. And not even having a batman.

"What, no car? No batman?"

I went on to tell him I could also do with a typist.

"I think we might find an ATS typist too," he said.

He was a man I could really warm to.

"It may take a little time," he said, "but don't give up trying to do what should be done within the Army, and do go through the proper channels."

When I got back to the flat that night, my cousin grinned at me and said, "I suppose you got a proper dressing down, telling off, chewing up, and spitting out."

"That's what you get from colonels," I said. "But generals are always gentlemen."

XVIII

Most Sunday afternoons were quiet in Hoechst; and I could feel a heavy autumnal stillness as I drove along its narrow high street. On either side the buildings of IG Farben towered, grey and ugly as prison walls. It was the dead hour after lunch had ended and before the world had begun to stir again. There wasn't a citizen or a soldier in sight. Ahead, the street curved and began to open out, leaving the factory grimness behind.

As the jeep swung round the long bend of the cobbled road, a girl stood by the roadside, maybe waiting to cross the street, maybe just standing.

There were always girls on the streets, hoping to pick up a boyfriend from the occupation army. It was a way of life, in which a vast surplus of German females tried to replace their three million dead menfolk. For them the soldiers of the occupation had the glamour of victors—also coffee, chocolate, and cigarettes.

Most German girls wore black, for many were war widows. The girl who stood on the kerbside wore a white dress, a big white wheel of a hat, and gloves milk-white against the golden flesh of her arms. There was something Sunday-ish about that gleaming and immaculate whiteness. It was almost as if she had just come out from church, she seemed so fresh and virginal.

The car bounced on the cobbles as I braked and came to a

screeching halt.

"Hello," I said. "Can I give you a lift?"

She came towards the jeep and I could see the long shape of her thigh and the easy rippling of the muscles of her legs. Her name was Maria and she was twenty two years of age, she told me in faltering English.

Inside my shabby bed-sitter I poured us each a glass of red wine, and we smoked a cigarette. Conversation wasn't easy, for we could speak little of each other's language. Other German girls I had met had all been a little hard somehow—with strident voice or a harsh laugh. The war had been tough on them; and there was a corresponding hardness within, as though they wanted to escape their sex and play the part of males. Maria, sitting there in my drab, sparsely-furnished room, was softly feminine.

"Prosit," she said as we sipped our wine, and "Danke schön" she smiled as I lit her cigarette. She sat, with her knees tight together, in the only armchair. Her skirt came just to her knees. Sitting opposite her on the edge of my iron-framed bed, I hardly knew whether to look at her legs which were so shapely, or at the straight-backed grace with which she sat on the edge of the chair, or at her smooth, quiet face with those dawn-grey eyes.

When we had finished the wine and stubbed out our cigarettes, we were at a loss for words. She gazed shyly around the room. It was a long, narrow room, with a high ceiling. The walls were decorated with some faded old-fashioned wallpaper, adorned at regular intervals with the print of pale and unrealistic roses. When her gaze returned to meet mine, I patted the iron bedstead and signalled for her to come and sit beside me. She smiled but didn't move. My gesture was meant only to reassure, but I saw she had mistaken it for the sexual demand all German girls expected of the victor.

In an effort to close the gap of strangeness and awkward silence which lay between us, I held out my hand to her.

"Ja," she said hesitantly—"I understand."

After a moment she rose slowly from the battered armchair and as she rose she looked even more beautiful.

She unfastened her dress and slid out of it in a white flash. Blushing, she turned sideways and beneath her slip removed her remaining clothes. With her back to me she shed her final garment, kicked off her shoes. Then she turned.

"Ich komme," she said. "Jetzt. Ins Bett."

We lay there for hours, the eiderdown removed, and our bodies embraced and made their own language of touch and feel and tenderness. We didn't need to speak until much later.

When she stroked my head and face with her hands, it was as though she was gathering words to tell me something.

"Du bist sehr schön," I said to encourage her.

"And you are like," she smiled—always that shy smile and those soft eyes—"der König von England."

My arm reached out to the bedside table and found a letter from home. I showed her the stamp on the envelope. "*That* is the king of England."

"Ja," she agreed happily, "and that is like you."

After that first visit she came every Sunday, arriving at exactly 2.30p.m.

We always drank a glass of red wine together. "Prosit," we said to each other. And when I lit her cigarette, "Danke schön" she smiled.

When we had drunk our wine, she would stub out her cigarette; and sitting on the bed, I would watch as she undressed herself to come and lie beside me. We made love in a score of different ways and never tired of each other. It was always easy and natural, tender and loving.

Afterwards, we would make ourselves a feast from the food which I had purchased specially for her at the Forces Exchange. It was not difficult to find there some dainty which was available to the Occupation Forces but was a forgotten luxury to German civilians. And when she left I always gave her the same presents—cigarettes "fur deinen Vater," and a small tin of coffee "fur Mutti." She would never stay later than nine-thirty, so that she could be home by ten, since this was the time her father had insisted that a respectable girl should be back.

He was a firm but kind man, I learnt from her. But he was now bedridden, and looked after by Mutti, and she did not wish to displease him. Both she and her young sister went out to work to support the family; I assumed that the father must have had a pension or at least some sort of disability allowance. But my inadequate German prevented me from learning such things more exactly.

At the time this barrier of language did not seem to matter. What did we need with words? I did not even know where she lived. For she would never let me take her home in the jeep, because she didn't want her fraternisation to become known to others. For this reason it always seemed natural that we met only in my room. During the week, I had my work; she had hers. Quite simply, we made no demands on each other beyond those few special hours each Sunday; and thus we lived in perfect freedom. I can't remember that in a formal way we ever arranged to see each other even on Sunday. I automatically assumed that Maria would come and she always did.

This regularity in her visits created a kind of fidelity into our relationship. Together with the undemanding nature of her attachment it led to a calmness which I had not experienced before. By comparison all previous relationships had been hectic, temporary, and in the end unsettling; but Maria remained a fixed constant. Frankfurt was her city, Hoechst her village. There she had survived the long years of war, the ghastly news of disaster from the Russian front, and now that the allies occupied her country she accepted their presence—and me with it.

The inter-allied personnel, girls who flocked from every
country of Europe to work for the Americans, came and went
like migrating birds. They stayed a little while, earned many
dollars and spent them, had 'a good time', burnt their fingers
in relationships that were unstable and impermanent. The
time and place undermined all their hectically constructed
foundations. Then one by one they disappeared. Most moved
back to the settled order of their own native land. Zara, Mollie, Michele, Dutch Julie, even Irene, ultimately migrated
homewards, their summer season ended. Angel waited on for
Dick and at long last they flew off together to the USA. The
men in uniform craved too for the accustomed certainties of
home, and lived for the moment of their posting or demob, un-
thinking and fatalistic.

My own demob date, too, was drawing near, and I had
begun to settle down with Maria, to await those regular Sunday visits, as though preparing myself for the calmer, more
domesticated world of peace ahead. For both of us it was an
interval of calm before things became once more as they had
been before the war. If such things could ever become quite
the same.

In Maria's attachment I found a fidelity which glowed as a
natural and comforting virtue. It did not aspire to a long term
end, but it would last for the duration of our relationship.
None of us could make our fairy tales last 'fur immer und
immer', but we could make something that would survive the
here and now, until the War Office moved this pawn or that or
swept it off its gigantic chess board altogether.

As the shortening days went by, autumn turning now to
winter, it never occurred to me that events in Maria's life
about which I knew nothing might cause any change. Her
personal history was so unknown to me that I was surprised
when she told me—since I had been curious enough to ask—
that her former lover had been a Nazi Storm Trooper. I found
it almost impossible to imagine one so delicate and tender,

learning the art of sex from (I imagined) some tough, jack-booted Nazi. She neither boasted of it nor was ashamed. As with all German girls, what had happened in the war seemed another, far-off part of their lives; something that had taken place, tender or sad, but now irretrievably past. He was only a boy, she told me; they had been at school together.

"What happened to him?"

She shrugged. "We were very happy. Then he was sent to the Russian front."

"Then?"

She looked at me for a moment, surprised that one should ask what happened to a man who went to the Russian front.

"Dead. Finished. Kaput." She turned to me quickly before some feeling of bitterness and fear, perhaps, could take possession of her. "But you are like the King von England. You not die, you live."

Whenever I tried to find out more about her, the language difficulty came between us, as well as a veil of reserve which she drew over her personal life. I already knew a little about her father and about her sister Lotte, who was younger than she by several years—"sieben jahre junger," she said. Although I made a point of always giving Maria some presents of cigarettes and coffee to take home, the only thing she asked me for had been for her sister. I'd wanted to load her with more cigarettes and more coffee, but she shook her head. Instead she moved to my dressing-table and picked up a small bar of chocolate. "Schokolade," she asked, "bitte? Fur meine Schwester?" Lotte, she told me, though young was very pretty, much prettier than herself.

"Nobody can be prettier than you," I said, proud that my German was improving. We practised it while we lay naked and warm in bed, and prompted by me Maria scribbled love messages in German on the faded old wallpaper.

One day, just before leaving for home, she said: "Next week I cannot come."

"But you must. Every Sunday."

"No, next Sunday I cannot."

"Every Sunday," I insisted.

"Tomorrow I go to hospital," she floundered. "Next Sunday I cannot come."

She tried for a long time to explain. I understood the word hospital, and I understood the word operation, but I could not understand the nature of the operation or the cause of it. She pointed to her stomach. "Der Magen," she kept saying. I pictured with horror the operating knife, and some insensitive surgeon's instruments probing into that live, responsive body. I couldn't imagine anything wrong with her, she seemed so perfect and so full of health.

"One week," she said as we kissed goodbye at the door.

In the street outside there was a little drizzle of cold rain. I gave her my raincape and she threw it over the shoulders of her white dress and ran off into the drizzle. She looked as virginal as on the very first day I had seen her.

I had a very busy week at work organising a visit by Charles Wilmot of the British Council. This was an important project in our educational liaison with the US. Charles was the brother of a Cabinet Minister and he himself a likeable and energetic man who was a pleasure to work with, but who necessarily took up my whole attention. There was little time to think of Maria.

On the following Sunday in the quiet stillness of midday everything seemed dead without her. I had a solitary lunch at the almost deserted mess and came back to my lodging feeling dispirited and irritable. Settling into the armchair in which Maria had sat on her first visit, I began to read an airmail copy of the *New York Herald Tribune*. The black iron-framed bed looked bleak and bare.

Outside, past the room's only window, a Polish guard paced idly along the street. It was a dull, grey day. I must have fallen asleep over the *Herald Tribune's* American news, for I was jerked awake into a flutter of alertness by a tapping on the door. The old tin alarm clock beside my bed showed half-past two. Maria, I thought, Maria had come—I must have completely misunderstood all those explanations.

I flung open the door—"Maria!" But it was not Maria. In the doorway stood a girl with curly hair and brown eyes. She was dressed in the usual funeral black, a two-piece suit with a black blouse buttoned up to the neck, which looked absurdly adult on one so young.

"Ich bin Lotte," she said. In her hand she held out my rain-cape. "Von Maria," she said. I took the cape automatically and led her into the room. We both seemed like actors playing a part in some drama of which we two were also the audience: our voices and our movements seemed detached from ourselves.

"Sit down," I said, and she sat in the armchair which Maria had always occupied. Her black skirt came just up to her knees, as Maria's white dress had done. "How is she?" I asked. Lotte looked blank, she shook her head.

"The operation?"

I pointed to my stomach, and moved my finger along it like a knife. Lotte shook her head.

I gave her a glass of wine. "Prosit," she said, just like Maria.

I lit her a cigarette. "Maria—Is she well?"

Lotte broke out nervously into fluent German. She was saying something about her Schwester, but what it was I couldn't tell.

"Why are you here, Lotte?"

She smiled blankly. "Prosit," she said again as she sipped her wine.

"Did Maria give you any message?"

She tipped her glass recklessly and drained the last of her wine. Then she stood up, and spoke slowly as she delivered her memorised message.

"Maria schickt ihre ganze Liebe."

Embarrassed, she ground her cigarette out quickly and half turning from me made a motion which stripped off her jacket. In another moment she had slipped her skirt down.

"Ich komme," she said approaching the bed, "anstatt—instead of—Maria."

"Nein, Lotte, es ist nicht—it is not necessary," I said blunderingly.

I grabbed my dressing gown and wrapped her in it. As I put my arms round her almost childish figure, she burst into tears and placed her head against my breast, like one who had failed.

I did what I could to comfort her. When she left I gave her the usual presents for father and mother and the usual chocolate for herself. And a small photo of me inscribed "to Maria with love, from 'der König von England'."

A few days later I received orders to report immediately to Hamburg for demob.

XIX

It was raining when I arrived in Hamburg, a cold winter drizzle which marked my last day in Germany before I reported
to the transit camp in the morning. By evening the rain had
cleared. I took a nostalgic stroll through the main streets and
it seemed like a repeat of my first days in Berlin. The pavements were full of slouching men in black with little bundles,
stationed in doorways or on street corners. They would accost
one with silken voices. "Excuse, please. I have underclothes.
Nice underclothes. You have frau back in England, or a
fraulein? She would like stockings, yes? What size please?
You tell me what size. I know English frauleins, they are very
tall, you want a big size. I have them, size nine and a half,
size ten; I sell you them for cigarettes."

There were young girls too, with voices more tense.

"Have you cigarettes? Listen, Tommy, I must have cigarettes. I will give you money for cigarettes. My parents need one
kilo butter, it will cost me five and twenty cigarettes. I give
you good time all night but I must take home one kilo butter.
You give me cigarettes, please?"

Everybody wanted cigarettes. Cigarettes were not a luxury
but a currency; and unlike the mark they retained their
value. When smoking a cigarette in the street, I had long got
used to being aware of a German shadow who would pad with
soft eager steps behind. Soon there would be two or three
more shadows. Toss away the fag end, and there would be a

165

dive and scramble. Then some lucky wretch would hold it up triumphantly, and scrunching it out thrust it into his pocket.

When I first arrived in the American Zone I remember discussing the black market in cigarettes with Johnny, the American billeted in the next apartment to mine, and an expert on the subject.

"First," he said, "you wanna get rid of that word blackmarket. Cigarettes is genuine currency; everybody uses them. What everybody uses, and everybody accepts, that ain't blackmarket. Besides, if I go without smoking and sell my cigarette ration to some guy who wants to give me marks for them, there's nothin' wrong with that, is there? It's just like any other deal, ain't it?"

"But *does* everybody want cigarettes?" I asked lamely.

"It's human nature," Johnny insisted. "There's nothing you can do about it, kid. Give a cigarette to a kraut and you watch him hesitate whether to smoke it or store it away. You wanta watch the expression on his face. It makes up for a lot that happened in the war. There's nothing they won't do for cigarettes—and that includes the dames. I tell you, you can sleep with any dame you like for half a dozen cigarettes, but you won't find a single dame who'll light up one of those cigarettes you give her. She'll crawl on her belly to get them and she may not have a strip on but she'll find her handbag and store them away in a flash. Have you ever tried chucking them a cigarette or two when they're in the nude? It's like chucking fish to the seals at the zoo."

"For Chrissakes, Johnny," I said, "it was conditions like this that brought about Hitler, and the Nazis, and the whole god-dammed war. We're trying to get the poor sods back on their feet, not grind them into the dirt."

Johnny laughed sourly. "They could stop it tomorrow. All they gotta do is call in the old currency and issue some new."

I wasn't up enough in economics to argue the point with him. I just wanted to know that somewhere somebody might be standing out against the prevailing hopelessness.

"Hasn't anybody ever refused your cigarettes?"

"Well," said Johnny, "there was that time I went to Berlin. I set out in the evening to take a walk round the place and see if I could pick up a dame. All along the main drag in every shop doorway, you could see them standing waiting to be picked up or maybe sauntering along kinda slow. It was ordinary stuff, like you might find anywhere. Me, I'm always on the look-out for something special. Then—Wham!—I saw this dame, real sexy she was, all dressed in black. A bit rough and rugged maybe, but looking kinda different from the others. I started walking along with her. She didn't *sprechen* any English and I can *sprechen* just enough Deutsch to get by, but not enough for social conversation. Anyways, after we walked for a time we get to her apartment.

"I take out my package of cigarettes. I hold out five to her. She shrugs. So I hold out ten. She shrugs again, kinda helpless. Fifteen? No response. 'That's the lot. Kaput. Finis,' I said.

"Then she started to tell me what she needed was not cigarettes but *kartofeln*—potatoes. In the Eastern Zone, she said, lived her sister and there they had many kartofeln. She herself had left the Eastern Zone and come to the west. But it was a mistake, here in the west was a shortage of *kartofeln*.

"I asked her why she didn't go back to her sister. I couldn't figure out her answer, but she kept insisting that she must have *kartofeln*. I held out all the cigarettes I'd got left and offered her the lot. She just pushed them away, and I thought to myself 'Why the hell did she bring me here?' While I was just getting kinda mad with her wasting my time like this, she takes me by the hand and leads me into the bedroom. 'Boy', I thought, 'you never know with dames. This is it.'

"It was a dingy, darkish room, with a large photo of her dead husband in his soldier's uniform on the dresser, and a double bed. She'd got hold of my hand and led me to the bed. Next I knew there I was, standing with her beside the bed,

167

gazing down at this pink-faced little Kraut asleep in his cradle.

"Boy, I got out of that place quick before she began talking about the kid needing *kartofeln* and her husband who was dead and my being there, and cigarettes not being what she wanted."

"So this was one time Johnny didn't get his girl?"

"Yeah, but lookit. If I'd had a sack of potatoes with me instead of cigarettes, or if I could have *sprechen* enough German to make her understand that she could use the cigarettes to buy potatoes, I guess there's nothing that dame wouldn't have done."

As I settled for the night in a large and one-time first class hotel on the edge of the lake Alster, I could not dismiss from my mind Johnny's boast about girls and cigarettes. The knowledge that tomorrow I would be leaving all this muddle and mess filled me with relief.

I awoke in the morning as excited as a schoolboy. The morning was bright and fresh and even in mid-winter seemed springlike, so that I wanted to run and dance and sing and even take a morning dip in the Alster, then eat a colossal mixed grill for my breakfast. I wanted to tell the world how happy I was to be going back home, finished with the army, leaving Germany behind and the occupation and the black market and all that went with it, the search for survival.

I opened my bedroom door, and a long thin arrow of sunlight streaked through the curtained windows along the quiet of the hotel's heavy-carpeted long corridor. From the next room there was the sound of male voices and laughter, as a German chambermaid came out into the corridor. Her blonde hair reflected the sunlight; her face was flushed. As she closed the door on the men's voices, their banter was still making her giggle; and as she saw me her smile spread as if to include my happiness with hers.

Her face, and her body as it moved, told what a wonderful thing it was to be young and alive even among the ruins of a half-shattered land. She came forward with the kind of confidence that is a challenge, and stopped a foot away from me. "I come to you now," she smiled, "to do your room. OK?"

She was a tall girl, and was almost level with me, face to face. Her breath smelt of warm, fresh brandy.

"Next door," she breathed, "they give me cognac to drink. Two New Zealand officers, they are very nice." Her eyes sparkled with almost childlike innocence and sense of fun; and her brandy-scented lips trembled delightedly. "They are very nice, they make love to me."

Confident with joy and cognac she threw her arms around my neck. The brandy taste passed from her tongue to mine.

"Now," she insisted, "I make love to you?"

Afterwards as she sat dressed before the mirror proudly combing her hair into place, I stood searching my pockets so that I could make her a present.

"Zigaretten?" I offered.

She smiled and shook her head.

As in a game, I tipped the loose cigarettes from the packet; they fell in long cylindrical snowflakes, dropping on her hair and her bosom and into the hollow of her lap. As she rose, laughing, they scattered in white abandoned patterns onto the red-carpeted floor.

At the door she turned and spoke. "Cigarettes? No, I like," she smiled.

Then she disappeared into the long corridor outside. I wished Johnny had been there to hear.

XX

The transit camp in Hamburg was a ghastly place, a shell-shocked building standing erect and gloomy amid the surrounding devastation. In its gauntness it had an uncanny resemblance to the Glasgow barracks where my army training had begun. Like a prison, its vast bare shell was surrounded by unscalable walls. Once inside, all you yearned for was to get out, in spite of the fact that tomorrow you would be embarking for home and a final release from uniform. Indeed, somewhere beyond the channel of the Alster, a berth along the wrecked dockside already awaited the boat which would bring us home.

Within the camp soldiers wandered, unfamiliar with its geography, like lost souls. Signs and directions were sparse and primitive. Everyone seemed transient, listless, unrelated. Kitbags and belongings lay everywhere, ready for sudden removal. Who stayed here? Who would wish to stay? No one it seemed, unless it was the adjutant.

In a vast and unadorned room which served as his office the adjutant sat amid piles of paper which cluttered his desk. He was rather young, blond, with tired lines in his face. "This'll be your shortest posting ever," he said to me cheeringly, as he had said to so many others.

"Fine. When do I leave on the blighty ship?"

"Report here tomorrow at 0900 hours and I'll issue you with your travel permit. Meanwhile enjoy yourself as best you can."

"Good," I said, "I think I'll go into town and see the sights for the very last time."

"That," he said, "you won't." He still looked weary but raised a little smile. "You may not know it, but once you are in this camp there's no going out. Sentries at the gates. Armed. The portals have closed behind you." Then to show that he was a public school man he quoted with his worn little smile, "*Facilis descensus Averni…* This place is like Hell, old boy, the entrance is easy…"

"But the exit well nigh impossible," I replied, showing I knew a bit of Virgil too.

He looked at me with a real grin this time.

"But why?" I said.

"Obvious, old boy. We've lost too many blokes that way, celebrating their last night in Germany. Too much to drink, German girls…"

Through my mind flashed the image of a blonde chambermaid smiling happily at the ruins of morality around her. 'No, I like', I almost found myself saying.

"Dark back streets," the adjutant went on. "Quite a bit of mugging. Chaps go missing. Records get in a muddle," he waved vaguely at the pile of documents on his desk. "No,—no, the orders are to stay in, old chap. Sorry and all that. Celebrate back in Blighty instead. You'll find the mess along the corridor outside, second left, first right. Like everything else in this place, it's not the Ritz. But at least tomorrow you'll be on board a British boat heading for Hull."

"Or Halifax," I said. He looked puzzled. "Hull, Hell, and Halifax," I explained. "If this is Hell, and I'm heading for Hull, what about Halifax?"

"No, no, old boy. You get your demob suit in Hull."

"I bet it's been *made* in Halifax then."

"Oh God," he said and waved again wearily at the pile of documents beside him. "I've got a heap of work to do keeping these records straight. Good luck tomorrow, you lucky sod."

It was the same for all ranks. The army had us all confined within the prison walls of the camp. I imagine the building had once housed the victorious German hordes in the same vice-like grip, except that they could have had passes out into town and other privileges, no doubt. Fair enough for one night. But hopelessly boring. There was nothing to do except find a book to read, have meals, sit in the mess with a drink in the evening and hope to find someone to talk to.

I began to look back on my tour of duty in Germany, seeing it as though for the first time. What an awful waste it began to seem. What had I achieved? What little good done, even if no harm? What Anglo-American goodwill had I secured? What benefit had been my presence to the shattered German economy, what helping hand had I stretched out to desperate German civilians? I had served my time, I had enjoyed myself whenever possible, I had done my duty. A little bit, perhaps, but somebody had to occupy the country.

Most of all I had survived. Yes, I had survived the U boats in the Atlantic, I had survived the bombings and rocket attacks on London, I had missed D Day and I had missed the Far East. Instead I had been sent to Germany, and even there I had survived the army bureaucracy. Or so I thought.

I was young and incredibly lucky. It may have been a waste of my youth, but it was better than lying dead on the Normandy beaches. Or missing in Burma like dear old Gully. Or shot down in the air years ago, like the Mexican boy George. I was lucky, a survivor—one who could look forward to the future. Above all, I was glad I was British with the proud hopes of a victor, and not a vanquished German. For what future had the German people now? Their lives seemed one big Kaput, they had gone down the road to ruin, and I could not see how they would ever come back.

Next morning after the list was called of those to report at the harbour for embarkation, I stormed into the adjutant's office. His pale blue eyes looked strained even in the morning light. "What's the trouble, old chap?" he said.

"My name's not been called for embarkation."

"Really?" He shuffled among the papers. on his desk, found the right sheet at last and read through it twice. "It seems your name's not on the list," he said with a kind of dismissive equanimity.

"Must be," I argued. "I was sent up from Frankfurt yesterday. A typing error perhaps?"

His little blond moustache twitched irritably. "First class typist," he said.

"But you told me nobody stayed more than one night."

"Not as a rule."

"Well?"

"Your papers can't have come through, old boy. Probably will arrive today, then you'll be on embarkation tomorrow."

"What! Another night holed up here?"

"Just bear with us, old chap. Should be all right tomorrow."

That was the army admin all over. Inefficient but hopeful to the last. The adjutant was a nice enough chap. Overwhelmed by paper though. I wished I'd asked him where he thought my papers were supposed to be.

"Your army records, old boy," he told me next morning when my name once again was omitted from the list. "We haven't got your records."

"What do you need with my records?" I asked. "I'm going to be *demobbed* My time is up, the army doesn't want me any more. I'm due out. Overdue in fact. Yet here I am stuck in this mainline railway station, where everyone is coming or going. Bar me."

The adjutant looked at me a little sombrely. "I'd get used to it, old man, if I were you. You see, we can't let you go without your papers."

"Well, where are they?"

"That's just it. BAOR hasn't sent them."

My God, I thought, the colonel's going to wreck my departure as he did my arrival.

"I wasn't stationed in BAOR. I was stationed with the Americans."

"Maybe," he said. "But without your army records we can't prove that. We don't know where you're from, actually."

"I've told you. I've come from US Army headquarters in Frankfurt. All you have to do is phone their I& E unit there and ask them to corroborate."

"Can't do that, old boy. It's not in procedures. I tell you what, I'll phone BAOR. Come back after lunch."

"Any luck?" I asked him after lunch.

"I spoke to the adjutant of your regiment there. Nice chap. Didn't seem to have any trace of you, though. He had a word with his colonel. Jolly decent, really. Off the record, the colonel didn't seem to know what we were talking about."

"Oh, he knew all right," I said.

"Sorry, they don't seem to have any trace of you."

"Does it matter? All I want is to be demobbed."

He looked serious. "Look at it this way. We don't know who the hell you are. You arrive here on your own, saying you're from the US Zone. We don't know. But we have to be careful. For all we know you might be a German."

"A German?"

"Yes. As far as we know, of course, old boy. No offence meant."

"What would a German do trying to get demobbed?"

"Dunno really. Infiltrate perhaps. Yes, infiltrate. You'd better hang on till we clear your identity. In the meantime report to this office each morning."

"Oh God," I said, "it's crazy."

"No, no," he answered reassuringly, "it's the army."

All the same I could see he was getting a bit irritated. At

the back of his mind perhaps there was a little niggle that maybe he was being tricked by some cunning German spy who had been to a British public school and knew Virgil.

"You've no documentation," he said sharply. "No identity. As far as the army is concerned therefore you don't exist. And we can't go round demobbing blokes who don't exist."

"I don't exist at BAOR, that's all. It's no good phoning them, they weren't supposed to have me. I was sent out by the War Office, and it was the Americans I was posted to. Why don't you phone the War Office in London and ask them if I exist."

I offered a silent prayer that the punched-hole card system still existed. If it did, then I did.

"Captain Hidden," sighed the adjutant. "If you were sent to Germany you must have been attached to BAOR wherever you went, whenever you went, and whatever you did there."

It was too complicated to tell him about the colonel playing his I-need-more-officers game. In my mind's eye I could still see him banging the telephone furiously and stomping round the office swearing he would not hand over the records of an officer stolen from him by the Yanks unless he was sent a replacement.

"You'll never get any papers from BAOR," I said, "unless you phone War Office."

"Can't do that, old chap. Protocol."

"Come on, take a chance. The war's over," I said. "Just phone War Office and ask for Brigadier Roberts." I gave him the Brigadier's extension number and hoped it still applied.

"Got a bit of influence there, eh?" said the adjutant respectfully.

"Just about enough." I managed to make it sound threatening.

"Right, I'll see what I can do. Report back at, say, 1600 hours?"

At four o'clock he was smiling and friendly again. "It's all been cleared. War Office has confirmed your appointment and BAOR will be sending on your details. You'll be able to embark tomorrow. Good luck, old chap, it's been nice to know you." He shook my hand and accompanied me to the door. "Tell you one thing," he said cheerfully. "You've set up a record."

"Record?"

"More nights in this place than anyone else. Except permanent staff of course. In the mess they were starting a sweepstake on how long you could last. No one else has been able to stretch it out beyond two nights. Thank God for that. My life would be impossible if all the others were like you. Ha, ha."

That night again I sat in the mess thinking over my time in Germany. Now that I was about to leave I realised how little I knew about the German people and what was once their country. In the Allied Compound we had lived cocooned lives, shuttered away for the most part from the homes and the family life of the defeated civilians. My own contact had been so peripheral that even Johnny the black marketeer knew more about them than I.

It was true that I would not exploit them by dealing in the black market. It was true that I would not wish to kick them off the pavement, as the French troops did not hesitate to do, if they didn't step aside on the approach of an Allied officer. But then they had not occupied my country. They had not pillaged our shops, raped or seduced our women, turned our men into collaborators, brought with them the peculiar moral evil of occupation. I could only feed my horror on what they had done to the Jews. As to what they had done to our cities by their bombing, our air force in the end had far surpassed that. In short all I had personally to resent was the waste of nearly four years of my life at a time when it might have been so much more creative.

I looked for something to put on the credit side of the balance sheet that I was so gloomily compiling as I sat there in the almost deserted mess. I recalled that I had tried to find out for my friends in London the whereabouts of several anti-Nazi families living in Frankfurt. There was, for example, one couple, an old man and his daughter who were living quietly in a small apartment in a side street. I conveyed my friends' messages to them, but then the language barrier prevented further contact. Yet in my visit to their house I saw an *ordinariness,* a normality, which contrasted with the frenetic activities of those other Germans I had met—the hangers on of the occupying forces, the whores and pimps and black marketeers; and the pathetic crowd of waiters and orderlies and laundresses and landladies and performing musicians and chauffeurs and shoe-shiners who all survived with studied servility.

What had I done that was any better, or indeed of any great value at all? Occupation of another people's country could never be any solution. It was not only the occupied who were corrupted through misery and tension, but the occupiers also. Yet, somewhere, I thought, good men were trying to make a future out of this all-encompassing waste. *We* were the minor nuts and bolts that held things in place while they got on with their reconstruction.

As we sailed from the still-scarred dockside down the Elbe towards the main sea, I had a clear picture from the boat's deck of how battered Hamburg had been. It took one's breath away. Three-quarters of the town's buildings, especially its centre and the dockside areas, had been wiped out by our blockbusters and incendiaries. Shipbuilding yards, factories, and warehouses were like newly made ancient ruins. In the river itself we passed ships, barges, even floating docks that still lay sunk or half sunk. It was heavier damage than I had seen at close quarters anywhere else, twice as bad as at Frankfurt, which, God knows, was bad enough.

I stood by the ship's rail and watched the broken city slowly recede, a city of shadows where a sad and defeated people hid themselves amid the rubble.

I did not foresee, could not imagine, that within a generation a new Germany would arise to become the leaders of western Europe. For I did not know then the resilience at the heart of the German people.

All I cared about was to arrive at Hull, throw off my shoulder tabs, get into the cheap demob suit and free flat cap or bowler hat they were offering me, and know at last that I was a civilian again, with all the precious freedoms and follies this might involve.

I remembered the Mexican George leaning over the rail of the Norwegian boat that had brought us to Britain. "For me," he had mourned, "it is the end."

Now, as the last sight of German land disappeared, I suddenly felt wildly free and shouted: "For me this is the beginning." Even the rush of the wind and the slap of the waves seemed to be helping not hindering, as our ship drove forward bringing us back to our dark serge suits and our bowler hats and our very own land at last.

BOOKS BY NORMAN HIDDEN

DR. KINK & HIS OLD STYLE BOARDING SCHOOL
"An alarming and clearly truthful book with its charming and touching end."
                                                            Sir John Betjeman

"Quite brilliant."
                                                            Laurie Lee

"A startling success as an autobiography."
                                                    Times Ed. Supplement

"One looks forward to future volumes."
                                                    British Book News

Paperback. 112 pages £4.90

SAY IT ALOUD: an anthology of poetry commissioned by The Poetry Society
"If you are looking for a fresh, wide-ranging anthology, choose this."
                                                    Spoken English

Hardback, dustjacket. 188 pages £5.95

HOW TO BE YOUR OWN PUBLISHER
a practical do-it-yourself guide.
2nd. edition. Paperback. 36 pages £1.80

FOR MY FRIENDS
One of the only two collections of Norman Hidden's own poems.
First edition. Paperback. 40 pages. A limited number of copies only. £4.95.

All the above books are available ONLY through
CLYDESDALE BOOKS.
No charge for packaging and postage in the UK if ordered NOW.

CLYDESDALE BOOKS
99 Pole Barn Lane
Frinton-on-Sea
Essex CO13 9NQ